# How to Buy and Sell a Business

# How to Buy and Sell a Business

Business

## A Practical Guide

**Barrie Pearson**
Livingstone Guarantee PLC

## DIRECTOR BOOKS

Published in association with the
Institute of Directors

First published 1995 by
Director Books
an imprint of Fitzwilliam Publishing Limited
Campus 400, Maylands Avenue
Hemel Hempstead
Hertfordshire, HP2 7EZ
A division of
Simon & Schuster International Group

The views of the author do not necessarily represent those of the
Council of the Institute of Directors

Typeset in 10/12½pt Palatino
by Dorwyn Ltd, Rowlands Castle, Hants

Printed and bound in Great Britain by
T.J. Press (Padstow) Ltd

British Library Cataloguing in Publication Data

A catalogue record for this book is available from
the British Library

ISBN 0–13–398926–7

1 2 3 4 5   99 98 97 96 95

To the directors, executives and staff of Livingstone Guarantee,
who deliver trust, personal commitment and outstanding
results to their clients.

# Contents

# Foreword by Clive Thompson

I recommend this book to directors and executives seeking an authoritative and practical guide to buying and selling businesses. The substantial experience that Barrie Pearson has accumulated, initially as a principal and currently as a professional adviser, is shared with readers and illustrated with actual examples.

The Institute of Directors have filled a need by providing sound advice to both buyers and sellers in one book. Buyers and sellers alike will benefit from knowing the approach and professional advice likely to be used by the other side.

# Preface

Most directors sell just one business during their career, yet the sharehold-ing is probably the most valuable asset owned by their family. So, to learn the process of selling a business by trial and error should be unthinkable. Equally, directors of listed companies are often given the task of buying or selling a business without training or previous experience, and conse-quently, many acquirers judge their acquisitions as much less successful than they had expected, when assessed with the benefit of hindsight. Mis-takes are always expensive – and sometimes disastrous. Unquoted acquisi-tions can be more complex and hazardous than deals involving much larger quoted companies.

This book has been written primarily for two audiences: shareholder directors of unquoted companies, who intend to sell their business at some stage; and directors and executives of listed groups likely to be involved in buying or selling a business. For whether buying or selling, it is invaluable to have an accurate insight into the likely approach and attitude of the other party. Practising accountants and lawyers too will find this book useful to obtain an overview of the whole process of buying and selling businesses, within which their professional expertise plays a part.

The entire buying and selling process is discussed, from the planning stage to successful legal completion. The main legal and taxation issues currently applicable are addressed, but expert advice in these areas is essential in every transaction. Regulations and controls have been ex-cluded, because these change frequently and out-of-date information is dangerous.

There is no magic formula to guarantee a successful acquisition or sale, let alone to ensure the success of the business thereafter. None the less, this book has been written expressly to increase substantially the chances of success. It is firmly based on first-hand and current experience of the challenges involved in buying and selling unquoted businesses.

* * *

Some special thanks are appropriate: to Ann Wilson for turning my ram-bling dictation into a finished manuscript, to Jeremy Furniss of Livingstone

Guarantee for checking the section on legal issues, and to Tony Bernstein of
H. W. Fisher & Co. for reviewing the taxation content.

Livingstone Guarantee,                                    Barrie Pearson
11–15 William Road,
London NW1 3ER

# 1 Planning for acquisition

Some people cut corners at the planning stage of acquisitions, yet arguably this is the most vital stage if you want to avoid making expensive mistakes and wasting management time. The outcome of the planning stage should be written down. If it is not, there is a risk that an acquisition will be made that is not in line with the planning that has been done, but human nature being what it is, this will be deliberately forgotten or rationalised away.

An example illustrates this point. A group asked corporate finance advisers to sell a subsidiary less than five years after acquiring it. The group was unable to find any written plan to diversify into this particular market segment and the managing director could not articulate any strategic reason for acquiring it, although he or she personally had authorised the acquisition. It was simply a case of ill thought out opportunism.

## 1.1 Strategic vision

A clearly articulated, written down strategic vision, setting out the chosen direction for the future development of the business, is an effective foundation for acquisition success.

The three key issues concerning acquisitions are the choice of:

- market segment;
- country or region;
- commercial rationale.

These issues will be addressed in turn.

### 1.1.1 Market segment

The choice of market segment is fundamental. It should be based on evidence, rather than on impression or instinct. The use of the term market segment rather than market sector is deliberate and important. For example, it is far too vague to decide to invest in the business to business services sector. This broad sector embraces dozens, if not hundreds, of individual market segments, with widely different relevance and attractiveness for any particular acquirer.

- Where the owners have ignored worthwhile expansion opportunities – e.g. to develop the business overseas – handsome returns may be achieved relative to the cash injection and management time involved.
- An opportunity to acquire a business with proven and entrepreneurial management, committed to develop the company profitably during the earn-out period because additional purchase consideration may be payable for achieving agreed profit targets.
- Monopolies and fair trading issues may be avoided simply because of the smaller size of the company involved.

## 1.3 Alternatives to acquisition

An acquisition of a business, with the purchase consideration paid in full on legal completion, should be the last alternative to be considered. While it is tempting to think that an acquisition will provide a shortcut to expand the business profitably, success is far from guaranteed. Consequently, the alternatives to be considered should include:

- organic growth;
- distribution and manufacturing agreements;
- a minority equity stake;
- a joint venture or consortium;
- a majority stake;
- an earn-out deal.

Each of these will be considered in turn:

### 1.3.1 Organic growth

Research shows that on average the equivalent of one executive year of management time is spent for each legally completed acquisition, before any post-acquisition work is initiated. This is a substantial amount of effort, which could be used to develop the business organically, and it is likely that the funds required for this will be significantly less than those needed to make an acquisition.

Whenever a business has the people available to develop and launch new products or services, or can recruit staff or possibly head hunt the nucleus of a team to do so, then organic growth merits serious consideration as an alternative to acquisition. If the market is growing rapidly or the company has been slow to enter a particular market segment, however, organic growth may take too long to realise an acceptable market share. None the less, organic growth should not be rejected. It must never be forgotten that post-acquisition success requires that effective organic growth is accelerated, and not merely maintained, in the business that has been acquired.

### 1.3.2 Distribution and manufacturing agreements

Distribution and manufacturing agreements may offer an opportunity to enter a market segment more quickly than by organic growth. Additionally, these agreements may provide an opportunity to achieve worthwhile profits and cashflow quite quickly, in return for a small initial investment. Equally, such an agreement may be a deliberate first step as part of a plan to make an acquisition approach to the company within the medium term. This might be a particularly effective way to get to know an overseas target company.

Some companies are justifiably wary of distributing products which are to be sold under the manufacturer's brand name. It has to be recognised that the manufacturer may terminate the distribution agreement when sales have been built up, and before the distributor has achieved an acceptable return on the cash and management time invested. Rather than reject an opportunity for this reason, an agreement should be negotiated which provides adequate protection for both parties. Key features to be incorporated include an adequate agreement period initially, followed by a sufficient period of notice if either party wishes to terminate the agreement. In this way, both parties should have enough time to make alternative arrangements.

### 1.3.3 A minority equity stake

There needs to be a good reason for deciding to acquire a minority equity stake. There is a danger that the acquirer will be locked in to an unlisted company without management control or even adequate influence over events. In these circumstances, and if the other shareholders are not prepared to sell the company, the only way to realise the investment may be to offer them the equity stake for purchase. In view of the danger of being locked in, a minority stake should not be regarded as a means of reducing the investment risk.

When a minority stake is acquired, the purchase agreement should provide:

- immediate board representation to provide the opportunity to learn more about the business and to influence future development;
- an option to acquire either majority or outright ownership within a given period, and at a defined price or valuation formula.

One sound reason for acquiring a minority equity stake is to secure distribution outlets, because it may be unnecessary to purchase the business in order to achieve this objective. For example, some building societies and insurance companies purchased large chains of estate agents primarily to capture the mortgage or insurance business. Generally speaking, these acquisitions have not been successful and some of the acquirers have since

Acquisition experience shows that sound reasons for acquisition include:

*To achieve market leadership, subject to monopolies, fair trading or anti-trust regulations which exist in the country concerned*

Evidence shows that market leadership, defined as having the largest percentage market share of any supplier, is likely to create the most profitable company in the sector. Obviously, market leadership should not be pursued to the point of diminishing returns. In many market segments, it would be nonsense to pursue a monopoly position by acquisition even if legislation allowed this.

*To increase market share in order to become a leading supplier, subject to legislative restrictions*

Some of the most successful acquisitive groups have a specific requirement that any acquisition should either be one of the three largest companies serving the market segment in the country or region, or provide the opportunity to achieve this goal within the short to medium term. Their commercial logic is simple and compelling. If a business is one of the three largest in terms of market share serving a particular country or region, it is likely to be visible to most prospective customers or clients.

Any prospective buyer is likely to know of or find out about the major suppliers and may well meet them in order to compare quality, delivery and price within the market. On the other hand, if the business acquired is merely a small player in a fragmented market, then regardless of the quality and value for money delivered, it may not be affordable to increase the visibility of the business sufficiently to prospective customers.

*To acquire a market leader in a niche business*

Although niche businesses usually command premium prices on acquisition, they often make successful acquisitions. A relatively small business may have the largest share within a country in a particular market segment, and large groups may find it uneconomic to attack this strong position.

For example, a printing group decided to buy a UK market leader in printing labels for major pharmaceutical manufacturers. This market segment is not easy to enter other than by acquisition. There is a technological barrier to entry because an element of security printing is involved. Pharmaceutical companies need to know the exact number of labels supplied so that every label is accounted for in their own production, in order to minimise the unacceptable risk of a bottle being labelled incorrectly.

As part of the security process, the pharmaceutical manufacturers buy small quantities of labels regularly. Consequently, the customer/supplier relationship is a long-term one and there is little incentive to buy pharmaceutical labels at a temporarily low price at the time of purchase. In sharp contrast, in some segments of the printing market customers are continuing to shop around for the lowest available price as there is still excess capacity available compared to demand.

*To broaden the product or service range, in order to offer an integrated solution to customers or clients*

A company providing office refurbishment decided to acquire a specialist window blind supplier. In this way, the product range was extended and the company was able to offer a more complete service of office refurbishment, partitioning, desk systems and specialist window blinds. Furthermore, the sales team were able to sell the enlarged product range effectively to the existing customer base.

*To diversify into an adjacent market segment*

It may be possible to acquire the necessary management, marketing and technical expertise together with a worthwhile market share from a single acquisition. In contrast, creating a similar business from scratch may take too long to create an acceptable market share.

*To penetrate a rapidly growing distribution channel*

Today, supermarkets sell a wide range of fresh flowers, pot plants, spring bulbs, and such like. Undoubtedly supermarkets will capture a significant share of this market from other distribution outlets. Consequently, it could make sense for a supplier which had failed to pursue this opportunity to catch up belatedly by acquiring a company which specialises in distributing these products to supermarkets.

*To protect a vital source of supply*

There may be a compelling reason to protect a unique or scarce source of supply by acquiring the business, but this is only likely to apply in a minority of cases. Even so, the alternative of acquiring a minority equity stake only should be considered first, because this could well provide comparable protection. In most cases, however, there may be considerable merit in retaining flexibility over the choice of suppliers in a changing world.

*To acquire assets cheaper and/or quicker than building them from scratch*

Where a company has entered receivership, or is struggling to survive, it may be possible to acquire ready-made assets on advantageous terms.

## 1.5 Value creation

There are very few opportunities in any market sector to make an acquisition at a sufficiently attractive price which will give an adequate financial return without the acquirer adding value to the new business. While it may be premature to create detailed post-acquisition management plans prior to legal completion – primarily because often there is insufficient opportunity to understand the business sufficiently – it is essential that outline ideas are identified and developed for value creation.

Ideally, the objective of any acquirer should be to accelerate organic growth post-acquisition, rather than merely to maintain the existing rate of growth. For example, it may be possible to expand sales nationwide in a business which has only served a particular region. Alternatively, it is quite possible that a private company has ignored the opportunities available overseas, despite having suitable products or services.

Another avenue for value creation is to unlock synergy post-acquisition. It may be possible to sell the products of each company to the customer base of the other. A careful assessment is needed to be satisfied that sales executives can effectively sell a wider product range. For a company building a nation-wide retail or distribution business, it may be possible to rationalise head office staff, advertising expenditure, distribution costs, and such like. None the less, many acquirers fail to recognise that there is usually considerable management time and expense involved before any synergy is unlocked.

Acquiring a loss-making business for a nominal sum and turning it back into profit may seem an obvious and attractive way to create value post-acquisition. In most cases, cost rationalisation alone may eliminate losses but is unlikely to deliver an adequate financial return on the investment in the medium term. Equally, doing more of the same is unlikely to be a recipe for success. Before acquiring a loss-making business, not only is it important to evaluate cost-saving opportunities, but the scope for introducing new products, widening the customer base and utilising different distribution channels must be assessed as well.

## 1.6 Overseas acquisitions

There are sound strategic reasons, both economic and political, for overseas acquisitions. Clearly, it makes sense to avoid undue dependence on the economy of one country. A recession in the home market may be at least partially offset by sales growth in overseas markets. For a company with a major share of the domestic market, or a retailer which has achieved comprehensive nationwide coverage, overseas growth may provide the only worthwhile opportunity to develop the business. Politically, a major business which is truly multinational is less vulnerable to threats from nationalisation. A number of major companies have moved their domicile and relocated their head office to a different country for political reasons.

There are serious risks and uncertainties in any overseas acquisition. There may be customer resistance and government reluctance to purchase from foreign-owned companies. Customer habits and shopping preferences may be quite different, and consequently products and packaging may need to be modified to suit the local marketplace. There is a possibility that this may only be realised as a result of post-acquisition experience, because the acquisition evaluation had not taken these issues into account. Ignorance of local regulations prior to acquisition may prove hazardous and expensive. A key factor contributing to successful overseas acquisitions is to remain in businesses in which the company has achieved success elsewhere.

An intention to acquire overseas requires particularly careful thought and analysis, before a decision is made or any target companies are evaluated. For some companies overseas acquisitions have proved to be nothing less than an expensive ego trip. Overseas acquisitions should be directly relevant to a defined corporate strategy. It is especially important that the alternatives to outright acquisition outlined earlier in this chapter are evaluated constructively, before making the decision to acquire overseas.

## 1.6.1 Selecting the country

Once the decision to acquire overseas has been made in principle, the next step should be to select the country. There is a trap for UK companies wishing to establish an overseas base in order to serve the European Union – namely, to imagine that the choice of country is not particularly important. This is simply not the case. When selecting a country for overseas acquisition, the key factors to be evaluated are:

- economic environment;
- cultural and social background;
- political stability;
- legal requirements;
- taxation and repatriation of funds.

These are considered next.

## 1.6.2 Economic environment

Ideally, the country selected should offer the following combination:

- a sizeable existing home market;
- adequate prospects for market growth;
- acceptable levels of inflation;
- a relatively stable currency.

It should be recognised that while the general prospects for economic growth in a country may be unattractive, it is quite possible that a particular market segment will offer an attractive investment opportunity, or vice versa. Impression, intuition and hunches are unacceptable ways of assessing economic prospects. There is no substitute for gathering and collating evidence. One starting point is to obtain surveys free of charge from banks, government organisations and embassies. If necessary, market research reports can be purchased or commissioned as a basis for making a sound decision.

### 1.6.3 Cultural and social background

In more remote parts of the world, it is important to assess the degree to which the country accepts overseas ownership of businesses. Evidence needs to be collected. Foreign investors may be treated differently from local investors. Some countries offer valuable financial incentives, while others impose restrictions designed to make foreign ownership less attractive.

The infrastructure needs to be assessed. Airports, railways and roads need to be sufficiently developed. While air travel directly to the capital city may be quite convenient, travel within the country may be time-consuming and uncomfortable. In these circumstances, there may be a sound case for restricting the location of any business acquired to within reasonable access of the capital or main airport. Communications and support services need to be adequate to support the business and keep pace with future development.

Local business practices and ethics may be quite different. The payment of bribes, from the petty to the substantial, may be essential to get things done or approved. Businesses may suffer from protection rackets, where payments are necessary in order to avoid trouble, and police action cannot be relied on.

The situation regarding expatriates must be assessed. Some countries will exert considerable pressure for expatriates to be replaced by local staff within the medium term. The safety of expatriate executives and their families needs to be considered. In some countries kidnapping is a hazard which cannot be dismissed. There may be an unacceptable threat of violence not only on the streets but in the home as well. Substantial insurance and costly security guarding of expatriates' homes may be essential.

### 1.6.4 Political stability

The possibility of local wars, civil unrest, political instability and national strikes must be assessed. The degree of stability within a country has a direct bearing on the payback period relevant for an overseas investment. To set up an assembly facility in rented premises, with little capital equipment required, may produce an adequate payback within as little as two or three years. For an acquisition, however, the payback period is likely to be significantly longer, so political stability is an important issue.

### 1.6.5 Legal requirements

Formal approval by a government agency is required in some countries for an overseas acquirer to purchase a business. Monopoly and anti-trust legislation may also exist. The local regulations must be understood at an early stage.

Restrictions on the extent of equity ownership by a foreign company may apply. In some countries equity control must be maintained by local shareholders. In these circumstances the key issue is management control. It may be possible to have effective management control while only having a minority equity stake. Consequently this could still prove to be an attractive investment opportunity.

Post-acquisition there will be local requirements to meet. The target company may come under the control of a regulatory body, which imposes onerous requirements on the business. Employment law may be quite different, particularly regarding termination of employment, and maternity benefits. Financial reporting requirements may be different. Local advice and information must be obtained as part of the evaluation of any country. It is unthinkable to adopt the attitude that one will make the best of the requirements and simply get on with the job post-acquisition.

### 1.6.6 Taxation and repatriation of funds

It is widely accepted that investment decisions need to be evaluated net of all taxes. Corporation taxation rates, allowances and incentives, tariffs, withholding tax and double taxation agreements need to be taken into account.

An adequate return on investment net of tax is not necessarily a sufficient financial justification to invest. The rules for repatriation of profits and capital may be restrictive. Particularly in a cash-generative business, it could mean that surplus cash generated is effectively locked up within the country concerned, and there may be no further opportunities to make an attractive investment locally.

### 1.6.7 Companies available to acquire

A country which may appear the preferred choice for acquisition could be ruled out because of a lack of sufficient target companies suitable for acquisition. Given that the owner of a private company may veto any acquisition approach, it is important that there are several suitable target companies in order to create the likelihood of making an acquisition at an acceptable purchase price.

If the company to be acquired is likely to be quoted on the stock market, then the objective should be to achieve an agreed bid. Therefore, there should be at least two or three suitable quoted companies. Unless the acquirer has made successful acquisitions as a result of hostile bids for listed companies, any thought of a hostile bid should be rejected at the outset. In these circumstances, the information about the target company that will be made available to the acquirer prior to legal completion is strictly limited, and the top management may be so hostile post-acquisition that the only acceptable response is to terminate their employment as quickly as possible.

### 1.6.8 Likely purchase price

Even if a country appears attractive and there are ample potential target companies, purchase prices may rule out that country for acquisition. An early check of likely purchase prices must be made to avoid abortive effort. An initial guide can be obtained by comparing price/earnings ratios for relevant companies in the overseas country with those in the local stock market of the acquirer. This comparison is valid for the planned acquisition of unquoted companies, as well as quoted ones, because relevant price/earnings ratios for listed companies have a strong bearing on the prices paid for unquoted companies.

Acquisitions made in the particular market sector and within the overseas country during the previous 12 months should be identified and available information collated. In this way, it may be possible to establish likely purchase prices and enable the bidder to decide at the outset whether these prices will offer an acceptable return on investment.

### 1.7 Defining an Acquisition Profile

The acquisition process necessarily involves abortive effort. Some of the most successful acquisitive groups examine as many as ten or even twenty businesses, for every one acquired. Some companies will be ruled out with minimal effort, following an examination of product literature and annual reports, while other prospective acquisitions will only be aborted after considerable effort, perhaps because of a failure to reach agreement at the final negotiation stage or as a result of unsatisfactory due diligence. It is because abortive effort is intrinsic to the acquisition process that everything possible must be done to minimise it. A vital tool here is the Acquisition Profile.

It is common today for subsidiary companies to be allowed to pursue acquisition opportunities. It should be made quite clear, however, that no target company should be contacted unless an Acquisition Profile has been agreed with a main board director. For good reason, strategic business plans rarely address acquisition intentions in meaningful detail. Without an appropriate Acquisition Profile, there is a risk that a subsidiary will seek specific approval to negotiate Heads of Agreement, only to be told by the main board that approval will not be given. This unacceptable waste of scarce management time should be avoided.

Acquisition Profiles are equally appropriate for private companies intending to acquire businesses. In the case of a sole owner, the Acquisition Profile should serve as a useful reminder of the type of business originally intended to acquire, because there is always the temptation to buy a business simply because it is available, or offered at an attractive price, even though it is different from what was originally envisaged. Where there are two or more owner-directors, there may be specific agreement to acquire, but differences of opinion may only emerge at a late stage in the acquisition process, when management time has been expended and professional fees incurred. An Acquisition Profile requires the owner-directors to think clearly and reach agreement on the type of business to be acquired.

An Acquisition Profile is a written description of the key features required in the company to be acquired. It should cover quantitative and qualitative features as appropriate, and even subjective aspects if these are important to the acquiring company. For example, some groups will rule out any loss-making business, and others will only acquire when the managing director will continue to be employed.

Brevity is important. An Acquisition Profile should not exceed two sides of A4 paper, and in many cases a single sheet should be adequate. The Acquisition Profile should outline:

- market segments, products or services;
- commercial rationale;
- maximum total purchase consideration;
- maximum cash available;
- minimum profitability and size;
- management;
- location;
- key features;
- financial return to be achieved.

Each of these will be considered in turn.

### 1.7.1 Market segments, products or services

A loose description, such as software businesses, is a recipe for wasted effort when pursuing potential acquisitions. More importantly, it is indicative of a lack of clear thinking.

The large number of software businesses currently in existence makes even the identification process unacceptably laborious unless the criteria are defined more rigorously. One way to reduce the number of relevant companies dramatically is to define the kind of application for which the software is designed; e.g., software designed for process control applications. A further reduction in the number of target companies could be achieved by defining the type of computer system for which the software was designed.

Whenever the initial definition of market segments, products and services produces an unmanageably large number of target companies, the criteria should be defined more tightly. Conversely, if the definition is so restrictive that only two or three target companies are identified, the range of acceptable companies needs to be reviewed, or it must be recognised that the probability of making an acquisition at an acceptable price is likely to be low.

### 1.7.2 Commercial rationale

A clear commercial rationale helps considerably to focus the acquisition search and minimise abortive effort. For example, the market segment may have been defined as the removals market, which would produce a large number of target companies. If the commercial rationale is to concentrate on high added-value services for major corporate customers capable of producing significantly above-average gross margins for the sector, the number of relevant companies will be much reduced.

### 1.7.3 Maximum total purchase consideration

In a group it is essential that a subsidiary should obtain approval of the maximum purchase consideration to be made available before any target companies are identified or approached. The amount of funds to be provided to a subsidiary for acquisition is a main board decision. A subsidiary should not assume that cash generated will automatically be made available for capital investment and acquisition. Equally, it would be wrong to assume that, provided the group target for the financial rate of return is achieved, unlimited funds will be available for acquisition.

The maximum total purchase consideration authorised by a quoted company should be based on cash resources, available borrowing facilities, the issue of shares and some form of loan stock as purchase consideration if appropriate. If the vendors are not prepared to take shares as purchase consideration, or only in part, it may be possible to arrange a placing of the shares with institutional investors on behalf of the vendors so that they receive cash at legal completion. Alternatively, it may be appropriate to have a rights issue of shares in order to raise the finance required for one or more acquisition. Loan stock could be an attractive form of payment to the owners of private companies, particularly for any deferred purchase consideration because the capital gains tax liability will not be incurred until the loan stock is redeemed for cash. In the meantime, it should be possible to negotiate a twice yearly payment of interest on the loan note at an interest rate comparable to current deposit rates, which will give the acquirer an interest reduction compared with overdraft rates.

For a privately owned company wishing to acquire, it is extremely unlikely that the vendors will wish to take shares as part of the purchase consideration. Even if a stock market flotation is planned within, say, the next 12 months, vendors should realise that it is not uncommon for stock market flotations to be delayed significantly, either because of disappointing profit performance or prevailing conditions in the stock market. Loan notes are unlikely to be an acceptable form of purchase consideration from a private company, because the vendors would undoubtedly wish the loan note to be guaranteed by a bank, and so the loan note would be a part of the borrowing capability of the acquirer, and not in addition to it.

On the other hand, venture capitalists may well be happy to finance an acquisition provided they are given the opportunity to purchase an equity stake in the enlarged business following acquisition.

### 1.7.4 Maximum cash available

When assessing the cash available for acquisitions, quoted companies should take into account the likely cash requirements of the existing business and the proposed acquisition over the next two years. Stock market experience has demonstrated that there have been periods in excess of 12 months when it has not been feasible to raise additional cash by a rights issue because of economic conditions.

Private companies should adopt a similar approach, but for different reasons. Cashflow is much harder to forecast accurately than profit. Furthermore, it is the inability to pay creditors which forces businesses into receivership. Shareholders in private companies should ensure that they maintain an adequate safety margin in their borrowing capability in order to avoid having to give personal guarantees to a bank for an increased overdraft facility to avoid going into receivership.

### 1.7.5 Minimum profitability and size

Some companies have an unswerving policy never to acquire a loss-making business because they recognise the risks involved and do not have suitably experienced executives to manage the business on a full-time basis immediately after legal completion. Other companies are even more restrictive, and will not buy a business which is just breaking even or only achieving unsatisfactory levels of profitability.

Quite understandably, the Acquisition Profile of many acquisitive companies will specify a minimum quantum of profit. Experienced acquirers recognise that a substantial amount of management time is required to legally complete even the smallest acquisition, and in practice there is an irreducible minimum of professional fees involved because there is a basic amount of work to be done in any transaction, regardless of size.

For companies prepared to buy businesses which are either loss-making or performing unsatisfactorily, minimum turnover is often an important requirement. Obviously, a larger turnover offers higher potential for profit improvement and often more scope for cost rationalisation than a smaller business.

Equally, it is preferable to make one sizeable acquisition, rather than two or more small ones, to achieve a similar market share. The management time and professional costs involved in handling only one transaction will be significantly reduced. The problems involved in integrating and rationalising two or more businesses will be avoided. Integration and rationalisation often involve removing surplus directors and persuading the remaining ones to accept somewhat different management roles. Operating systems and procedures will inevitably be different, and some harmonisation will be necessary. This could be a deceptively long-winded and time-consuming process.

### 1.7.6 Management

Few companies are prepared to acquire successful private companies and agree to the managing director leaving at legal completion. Businesses are particularly vulnerable to a change in ownership, and this is compounded when the managing director leaves at the same time. On the other hand, when a business is loss-making or performing unsatisfactorily it is important to install a suitably experienced executive immediately on legal completion.

If an acquisition is to be successful, it is essential that the values, styles and culture of the two management teams are compatible. This is not to suggest that they should be identical. Imposing changes in the management culture of a successful business post-acquisition may prove to be damaging. Not only may the owner-directors leave prematurely, but some key executives and managers may leave too and perhaps be recruited by competitors. On the other hand, when a new managing director is appointed to turn round a loss-making business there is a strong case for adopting the group culture as a matter of urgency.

Budgets, monthly management accounts and regularly updated, year-end forecasts will need to be prepared in a standard format, within the timetable set by the group. To help achieve this smoothly, adequate training and guidance should be provided by the acquiring company. With regard to other systems and procedures, successful acquirers recognise that standardisation can be counterproductive and a flexible approach is a valuable aid to success.

A significant proportion of private company acquisitions involve an earn-out deal, where the vendors have the opportunity to earn a significant additional payment in return for achieving improved profits in the two or three years following acquisition. Acquirers should recognise, however, that the overwhelming majority of owner-directors leave the business at the end of the earn-out period or shortly afterwards. Consequently, acquirers should implement a definite programme during the earn-out period so that the personal contacts and expertise of the owner are not lost when he or she leaves the business.

### 1.7.7 Location

The location of a potential acquisition within a country is a practical rather than a strategic matter, but is nevertheless an important one. It makes sense to think in terms of travelling time rather than distances. A journey time of up to two hours means that people can visit the business acquired, do a full day's work and avoid the cost and disruption of an overnight stay.

### 1.7.8 Key features

Some companies' Aquisition Profile lists so many essential features required of the target company that, unwittingly, they have described a perfect business. None exists. Although such an Acquisition Profile is designed to avoid failure, it is a recipe *for* failure because all the available target companies will be rejected.

Only two or three key factors should be identified, and each of these regarded as essential for success. It is important that these key factors should be complementary, rather than similar to the strengths and weaknesses of the acquiring company. If a target company is weak in a key area where the acquirer has demonstrable strength, it should be possible to inject the necessary expertise. But if the acquirer is just as weak in that area, this could prove to be a real difficulty. Key factors for success should only be defined on the merits of the particular case and the circumstances of the acquirer.

For example, a key factor for success required by a soft drinks manufacturer may be a concentration of sales to supermarket chains, because the existing business is too dependent on supplying the cash-and-carry trade and catering outlets; alternatively, another company could understandably be concerned at the over-dependence on one particular supermarket chain. The key factor for success is a business which trades primarily with other supermarket groups.

### 1.7.9 Financial return to be achieved

An Acquisition Profile is incomplete unless the financial return to be achieved within a given timescale is defined. This can be expressed in a number of ways – for example, a required discounted cashflow internal rate of return, a minimum return on the net funds invested in the second financial year after acquisition, or a multiple of after-tax profits calculated either on the previous year or the current one. Additionally, a minimum figure may be specified for the percentage on net tangible asset backing in relation to the purchase price at the time of legal completion. Valuation is discussed in Chapter 6.

## 1.8 Key point summary

1.  A rigorous choice of a particular market segment at the outset, rather than merely a broad market sector, is fundamental to success.
2.  Alternatives to outright acquisition should always be evaluated before deciding to proceed.
3.  The choice of country for overseas acquisition should be rigorously evaluated at the outset.
4.  An approved Acquisition Profile focuses the acquisition search and minimises abortive management effort.
5.  The objective of any acquirer needs to be to accelerate profitable growth post-acquisition in order to achieve an adequate financial return, and outline ideas need to be formulated before legal completion.

# 2 Planning a sale

Listed groups generally make a conscious decision to initiate the sale of a subsidiary, although their preparatory work and planning of the sale process sometimes lacks rigour. On the other hand, the sale of a significant number of private companies is usually triggered by an unsolicited approach from a prospective purchaser.

Careful planning is needed to maximise shareholder value, not only to ensure that the transaction is handled effectively but also to carry out preparatory work prior to the initiation of the sale process. Planning for a successful sale requires that the following issues are addressed:

- valid reasons for selling;
- alternatives to an outright sale;
- timing the sale;
- obstacles to selling;
- preparatory work prior to sale.

Each of these issues will be considered in turn.

## 2.1 Valid reasons for selling

When a valid reason for selling arises, it should not be ignored. A lengthy delay in initiating a sale may significantly reduce the value that can be realised and in extreme cases may make the business unsaleable.

Some valid reasons for sale apply primarily to subsidiaries of listed groups, others mainly to private companies, and some are equally valid for both. The following circumstances need to be recognised and evaluated:

### 2.1.1 Forthcoming retirement

Business owners should not wait until they are approaching retirement age before initiating the sale of their business. The retirement of an employee occurs automatically at pensionable age, but selling a business is not nearly as simple or as assured. If a market sector is affected internationally by a recession there may be no buyers prepared to pay an acceptable price for the business, and this situation could last for as long as three years.

During the recession of the early 1990s, there were no buyers internationally prepared to pay sensible prices for media services companies, because the prime concern of companies was to concentrate on the profitability of their existing businesses and avoid breaching banking covenants.

Generally, there is a strong case for initiating the sale of a business before the shareholders reach the age of 60, especially if there is likely to be an earn-out period of two or three years before the final purchase consideration is received. Many business owners discover they work longer and harder during the earn-out period than they ever imagined possible.

### 2.1.2 Retirement relief

Under present rules in the UK there is a valuable capital gains tax saving available to shareholders working full time in a private company provided they are aged at least 55 at the time of the sale. Consequently, it may make sense to delay a sale in order to take advantage of this tax relief. Before making any decision, however, the shareholders should take professional advice to assess their eligibility and the amount of tax saving in their particular case.

### 2.1.3 Ill health

There is inescapable actuarial evidence that people over the age of 45 become increasingly vulnerable to unexpected and lengthy illnesses, or even sudden death. Faced with deteriorating health, it could make sense to initiate a sale rather than allow performance to decline gradually because of a lack of effective management within the business.

### 2.1.4 Lack of enjoyment and enthusiasm

This may seem a surprising reason to put forward, but it is a valid reason for selling. Many people start a business while still in their late twenties, and so have spent 20 years working in the same business by the time they are in their late forties. Not surprisingly, enjoyment and enthusiasm sometimes wane. Difficulties caused by coping with a recession, the problems of managing and motivating staff, legislative changes and increasing competition all take their toll. When enjoyment and enthusiasm for the business are lost permanently, and not merely temporarily, it is a danger sign. The business is at risk of going into a decline. In these circumstances, there may be a strong case for selling.

### 2.1.5 Cashflow crisis

Particularly in difficult trading conditions, listed companies may overborrow and face the prospect of breaking banking covenants. In these circumstances, the sale of a subsidiary may be appropriate. Ironically, it may be necessary to sell one of the more successful subsidiaries in order to raise sufficient cash and be assured that a legally completed sale will be achieved.

Private companies are more vulnerable to cashflow problems than are listed groups. When overdraft limits have been reached and other avenues for borrowing exhausted, the only way to obtain additional borrowing may be for the shareholders to give a personal guarantee to the bank, a choice they may regard as unacceptable. In these circumstances, selling the business may be appropriate. If the cashflow problems are sufficiently serious that there is a risk of receivership, there is a strong case for initiating a sale as a matter of urgency.

To delay a sale in the hope that the problem will be overcome may literally be gambling using the value of the business as a stake. Worse still, if the shareholders have given personal guarantees to the bank or in connection with a lease, they stand to lose not only their business but their home as well. Once prospective purchasers realise or sense that a business faces the risk of receivership, they are likely to drag their feet in order to allow the business to fail or to negotiate a savage reduction in the agreed price prior to legal completion when the only alternative for the vendors is receivership.

### 2.1.6 Increasing competition

As business becomes increasingly international, and even global in some market sectors, the threat of increasing competition from major overseas companies is a reality for both listed and private companies. A sizeable and privately owned distributor faced such a threat. Several major overseas manufacturers were intent on setting up their own distribution businesses in the UK, rather than merely supplying to local distributors.

The favoured method of entry into the UK was by acquisition, and companies were prepared to pay a premium price to acquire a suitable business. The owners faced a simple choice. They could either accept a premium price for their business today, even though they had not anticipated selling in the foreseeable future, or face an inevitable decline in profitability as major overseas producers entered the market. Understandably, they chose to sell.

### 2.1.7 Legislative change

European Union legislation is having a significant effect on businesses in some market sectors. For example, the stringent conditions imposed on food manufacturing businesses means that some private companies are unable to make the necessary capital investment or achieve an acceptable profit subsequently. In these circumstances, a sale may be appropriate.

### 2.1.8 Declining market demand

Fashion and taste are changing more rapidly then ever – for example, for some years now, sales of red meat in Europe have been declining and this is unlikely to be reversed. It may make sense to sell a business that is in an inevitable decline rather than wait until the business has become unsaleable.

### 2.1.9 Technological change

Some private companies realise that technological change is leap-frogging them, but the level of investment required is prohibitive. If the problem cannot be overcome in any other way, the business should be sold.

### 2.1.10 Non-core businesses

Groups of companies change their strategic focus and direction occasionally to reflect changing market conditions. Subsidiaries may become non-core or peripheral to the mainstream activities of the group. In these circumstances, it is inadvisable to adopt the attitude that because a subsidiary is making a tolerable level of profit a sale should be postponed. There is every likelihood that the group will be reluctant to invest sufficiently in the business to keep pace with competitors who are committed to the sector, and gradual decline will be inevitable. Furthermore, the most talented executives and staff will recognise that the group is no longer committed to the business and may leave, thereby accelerating the decline.

### 2.1.11 A loss-making business

Listed groups are as prone as the owners of a private company to seek to sell a loss-making business. Before deciding to sell, however, a realistic assessment should be made of the likely profitability which could be achieved over, say, the next two years. A valuation of the business today should be compared with its likely value in two years' time. This allows an objective decision to be made as to the additional value achievable by turning the business round prior to sale. Also, the number of likely purchasers will be higher once the business has returned to profitability because a significant number of companies will not consider acquiring a loss-making business.

## 2.2 Alternatives to an outright sale

Many owners of private businesses, and some listed groups, regard the only option as 'to sell or not to sell'. Before deciding to sell a business to corporate acquirers, there are several alternatives which should be considered, even if only briefly. These include:

- buying back own shares;
- selling a minority equity stake;
- a merger;
- selling to a management buy-out or buy-in team;
- a flotation on the stock market.

Each of these alternatives will be considered in turn.

### 2.2.1 Buying back own shares

In some private companies, one of the shareholders may be approaching retirement age but the other shareholders may be much younger. They are likely to be reluctant to sell the business simply to allow one shareholder to exit. Present legislation allows a company to purchase its own shares for cash. The company must have the power to do so incorporated in its Articles of Association and must be authorised by a Special Resolution of shareholders. The purchase price must be available from retained profits which are available for distribution to shareholders. Also, payment must be made in full and in cash, but the company may borrow the money to make the payment. Usually, the purchase of shares will attract Advance Corporation Tax and this must be taken into account in the cashflow planning. Expert advice should be taken at the outset, and the starting point for advice should be to consult the company's auditors.

### 2.2.2 Selling a minority equity stake

Another alternative which retains management control of the business for the shareholders is to consider the sale of a minority equity stake to one or more financial institutions. This could be used to allow a retiring shareholder to exit and receive cash for his or her shares. Alternatively, several shareholders could be given the opportunity to sell some of their shares, provided they can satisfy the financial institution that they are committed to achieving continued profit growth.

Sometimes shareholders in a private company are persuaded to sell a minority equity stake or, worse still, grant an option to acquire a minority equity stake, without sufficient thought, in order to obtain additional loan finance. Every effort should be made to obtain sufficient loan finance, without having to sell equity on unfavourable terms. Some private companies have only discovered years later that they granted share options in order to secure loan finance and gave away a large capital sum because the company succeeded beyond their wildest dreams.

The sale of a minority equity stake to a corporate acquirer or trade partner may have a serious impact on the prospects for selling the business later. Almost certainly, the minority shareholder will have protection in the form of pre-emption rights providing the opportunity to purchase the other shares in the company at the same price as a potential bidder is prepared to pay. Given this situation, it is entirely possible that no acquirer will make an offer because it is assumed that the minority shareholder will always match the price. In effect, the sale of a minority equity stake may have pre-selected the only prospective purchaser for the business.

Furthermore, it should be realised that when a potential trade buyer acquires a minority equity stake in an unquoted company, it may well be conditional on options in the legal contract to acquire either management control and/or outright ownership within a given period. When this approach is adopted, it is quite commonplace for the purchase price of the remaining equity to be defined in the legal contract by specifying the valuation formula to be used.

When an institution acquires a minority equity stake in a private company, it is usual for the institution to nominate a non-executive director. Some institutions have a policy of always appointing the executive who made the investment on their behalf, while others choose someone from their register of available non-executive directors.

Some private companies dislike the thought of having a non-executive director imposed on them, who they anticipate is likely to interfere and will be a spy in the camp. Rarely are these fears justified by experience.

The institutional investor should be asked to provide a non-executive director who can provide relevant skills and experience to complement existing board members. For example, someone with a specialist knowledge of foreign currency management or establishing overseas sales offices in mainland Europe could be particularly appropriate to the future development of the business. Alternatively, someone with relevant industry experience gained from a different perspective could be helpful. The person may have experience in the industry at either the customer or supplier end of the chain, which could bring a valuable perspective and insight to the company.

A rapport between existing board members and the non-executive director is essential. If the institution plans to appoint the executive handling the investment and a rapport is not established, a tactful request should be made to have another executive appointed from within the institution. If the first candidate from a pool of non-executive directors is regarded as unsuitable, a request should be made to meet an alternative candidate.

Non-executive directors often bring tangible benefits to private companies. They help achieve a more structured approach to board meetings, which can be a useful discipline, and may have particularly useful personal contacts among prospective customers and suppliers. This potential benefit is one many private companies do not exploit adequately.

### 2.2.3 A merger

The merger of two private companies, without any exchange of cash, may seem an attractive idea and could be seen as an effective way of overcoming a business problem. The reality is that very few of the proposed mergers of private companies are legally completed.

The prime cause of attempted mergers not happening is a failure to agree on valuation. The two prospective partners have to agree the percentage of the merged company that each will own. Unlike quoted companies which have established market share prices, there is no similar benchmark in the case of private companies. Even if shares in a private company have changed hands recently, it may well have been between related individuals and not necessarily at full value.

The difficulty is to reach agreement on the equity split. This requires taking into account future profitability and cashflow generation, the net asset value of each company and performance to date. Often, the difficulty of reaching agreement proves insurmountable. None the less, there could be valid reasons for seeking a merger:

- to accelerate a stock market listing by reaching an acceptable level of profit more quickly;
- to create a sufficiently large business to support the minimum level of infrastructure, distribution network or research and development needed in order to compete effectively against major companies;
- to overcome problems caused by sudden death, serious ill health or enforced retirement, when the timing for selling the business is unsuitable;
- to reduce undue dependence on a particular customer, product or service.

It is not enough to reach agreement on the equity split between the two sets of shareholders and then to proceed to legal completion. The future direction, priorities and goals of the merged business need to be agreed prior to legal completion. Ample time must be invested in discussion to reach this agreement, and the outcome should be written down in the form of a concise business plan to avoid misunderstanding and disagreement later.

There should be only one managing director after the merger, because joint managing directors rarely work together effectively. Some of the existing board members may need to retire or resign in order to avoid burdening the new business with onerous overheads. The role of each director in the merged business must be discussed and agreed. Each director should have individual accountability, not a shared one.

Salary levels, bonus systems, fringe benefits and conditions of employment for shareholders, managers and staff need to be addressed in broad terms prior to legal completion. The problems of unifying these arrangements and the management time involved should not be underestimated.

Additionally, there may be a need to rationalise office or production facilities. It may be considered necessary to change the name of the business, which means redesigning product literature, changing vehicle livery, stationery, and so on. The result is that while a merger may seem a good idea, it may not be deliverable and in any event is likely to be more costly, time-consuming and onerous than anticipated. It may make more sense to obtain financial backing to acquire another business to achieve the same objectives as a merger would have done, even if it is necessary to sell an equity stake to an institutional investor in order to obtain the finance.

### 2.2.4  Selling to a management buy-out or management buy-in team

A management buy-out involves several members of the management team, financed by one or more institutional investors, buying the company which employs them from the shareholders. While the majority of management buy-outs have involved subsidiaries or divisions of listed groups, and this will undoubtedly continue to be the case, a significant number of transactions have involved the purchase of private companies.

Management buy-ins involve two or three executives buying a company in an industry sector in which they have worked, usually having run a significantly larger business. Buy-ins are financed in the same way as buy-outs.

It may appear a particularly attractive option to sell a business to a management buy-out team rather than a trade buyer, by rewarding the loyalty of the people who have helped to build the business with the opportunity to buy it. There is a probability, however, that trade buyers may be prepared to offer a higher price because they have the opportunity to unlock synergy post-acquisition by rationalisation or integration with another business already in their group. It must be realised that institutional investors will not match the price offered by a trade buyer simply to avoid losing an attractive investment opportunity.

The price offered by any institutional investor will be calculated to ensure that a target annual rate of return is achieved during the period from investment to eventual exit by sale or stock market flotation. It should be recognised that many trade buyers are not prepared to compete against a management team to buy a business, because they do not wish to risk inheriting a demotivated management team who may leave shortly after the acquisition.

It must be realised that the probable outcome of a management buy-out or buy-in will be a sale or flotation of the business within 3–5 years. Consequently, vendors should ensure that the timing and the realisable value are attractive, and that a sale of the business is not being pursued prematurely.

There is no place for sentiment when considering a buy-out or buy-in, or when dealing with a management team after permission to pursue a buy-out is given. Management should be regarded and treated as just another prospective purchaser. Buy-outs and buy-ins are undoubtedly a complex area for both vendors and management teams. Chapter 9 is devoted to the subject.

## 2.2.5  A flotation on the stock market

Not every company of sufficient size is suitable for a stock market flotation. The process of obtaining a listing is time-consuming and costly; having experienced it, some directors would describe it as tortuous. Furthermore, there are obligations and restrictions placed on the directors of listed companies. Consequently, it will be appreciated that a decision to obtain a stock market listing requires considerable thought, analysis and preparatory work.

The Official List is the main market regulated by the London Stock Exchange. To justify the management time, expense and obligations involved in a flotation, the market capitalisation or worth of a business to be floated should be a minimum of about £20 million. The Unlisted Securities Market, which was designed to allow smaller companies to obtain a stock market listing, will end on 31 December 1996. Alternative arrangements are to be introduced for smaller companies, but it is too early to assess how effective a market in the shares this will provide.

There are benefits to be gained by shareholders, executives and staff as a result of a stock market listing. These include:

- The shareholders will retain management control of the business and have the opportunity to sell up to about one third of their shareholding at the time of the flotation. They will be required to retain the majority of their shareholding at flotation to demonstrate their commitment to the future success of the company.
- A realistic market price will be created for the shares, which can be bought and sold more readily.
- Additional finance will be available by creating more shares. A rights issue could be made to existing shareholders, underwritten by financial institutions so that there is no obligation on existing shareholders to subscribe for additional shares. The issue of shares may be used to pay directly for acquisitions, by placing them with institutional investors so that the vendors receive cash at legal completion.
- Financial status may be enhanced significantly. Multinational customers and suppliers are more likely to be concerned about the financial stability of a private company than one listed on a stock market.
- Corporate and public awareness of the business is likely to be increased by press coverage leading up to a stock market listing, and the continued interest in the performance of the company afterwards.
- Management and staff motivation is likely to be improved.

The prospect of a flotation often creates excitement within the business. Staff with a shareholding will have the opportunity to sell a proportion of their shares at listing, and others may have an opportunity to buy shares. Share purchase and share option schemes can be introduced to provide attractive and cost-effective incentives for management and staff, and these help focus efforts towards the future success of the company.

For a company to obtain a stock market listing, an experienced management team and future profit growth throughout the medium term must be demonstrated to the stockbroker or merchant bank which will sponsor the flotation. The reputation of some sponsors was damaged during the early 1990s by newly listed companies failing to perform as well as expected, which has resulted in a significant decline in the value of the shares compared with the listing price. The sponsors will carry out a rigorous investigation of the history and prospects of the business, with the help of an investigation by a major accountancy firm, which will be asked to produce what is known as a long form report on the business.

The sponsor will want to be satisfied of:

- satisfactory profit growth in recent years;
- adequate budget, management accounts, profit forecasting and cash management to ensure current year forecasts are reliable;
- a sound business plan demonstrating adequate profit growth during the next three years and a long-term future for the business;
- no undue dependence on one person, or a single product, service or mere handful of customers or clients;
- the finance director is a suitably qualified accountant;
- the auditors are a major firm, or a well-respected, medium-sized one, or will be changed before flotation;
- corporation tax, PAYE and VAT matters are in order and up to date;
- adequate cash will be available for working capital and capital investment, without the need for a rights issue in the foreseeable future;
- there is no major litigation in progress or threatening the company.

Although a stock market listing can take place within about four months, many companies may need between 12 and 18 months in order to get the company into suitable shape for a listing. Without question, there will be several months of intense effort. It is strongly recommended that only two directors are closely involved with the provision of information for the long form report and the drafting of the prospectus. It is essential that the preparatory work does not distract the board during the vital period prior to flotation, which could result in the failure to meet the expected pre-tax profit in the year of flotation.

Some recently floated companies have suffered in this way, and the decrease in share value is likely to be markedly greater than the profit shortfall. Furthermore, investors are unforgiving in these circumstances and have long memories. It may take several years, despite subsequent profit growth, before investors are prepared to value the shares fully again.

Whereas in private companies a more relaxed and annual view of profit performance is quite commonplace, listed companies are required to report their financial results at six-monthly intervals. Investment analysts and financial journalists not only compare current year performance against the previous year, but make the same comparison on first half-year performance. This creates additional pressure on the directors, management and staff of the business to achieve a satisfactory profit performance every six months.

Many private companies either do not pay dividends or do so only intermittently to meet the financial needs of shareholders. Investors in quoted companies, however, have an expectation about the yield they expect to receive from dividends in relation to the current value of the shares. Also, shareholders expect the purchasing power of their dividends to increase annually. So there is a significant drain on cashflow for any quoted company which must be taken into account.

Directors of listed companies must realise that they will be subject to continuing public scrutiny. Directors of some private companies enjoy indulgences paid for by the business which will be completely unacceptable to the sponsors. A company boat, an aeroplane, an overseas villa and other extravagances such as racehorses will need to be owned and paid for by the director before listing.

The regulations and timetable of events laid down by the Stock Exchange need to be strictly adhered to. Annual general meetings become a formal and public occasion, and the directors may face hostile questions on contentious issues. Directors are not allowed to buy or sell shares at various sensitive times during the financial year, and whenever they buy or sell a significant number of shares this is likely to attract press comment and speculation.

Journalists are always looking for stories about listed companies. Unfavourable stories are as readable as favourable ones, if not more so. A story about a listed company may appear in the national press and adversely affect the share price, which would not have attracted attention if the company had still been private.

One method of obtaining a stock market listing which creates undue interest is the possibility of reversing into a shell company, but this is only recommended for a small minority of companies wishing to list. A reversal involves a small listed company acquiring a private company by issuing primarily shares rather than cash, with board control of the enlarged listed group being handed over to the directors of the private company. There is no need for the listed shell company to be in a similar business to the private company being acquired.

None the less, it must be recognised that formal Stock Exchange approval must be obtained. Most reversals into a listed company involve either a private company which is not large enough or suitable to obtain a listing in the usual way, or a management wishing to obtain a stock market listing to create a vehicle for financing rapid growth by acquisition. Suitable listed companies for reversal are likely to have a majority of the shares controlled by one family or members of the board, which makes it easier to sell the idea.

There is always the risk that the shareholders will push up the share price before buying the private company in order to give away a smaller percentage of the equity, and the shareholders in the private company lose out accordingly. The other danger is that there may be serious problems in the business of the listed shell company, which the private company may not have the opportunity to investigate sufficiently for comfort.

The reality is that if a private company is suitable for a flotation, maximum shareholder value will be realised by obtaining a listing rather than by reversing into an existing company.

## 2.3 Timing the sale

The first step is to evaluate the alternative exit routes described in this chapter before deciding that a sale to a trade buyer is the preferred route. Then the question of timing must be considered. Listed companies contemplating the sale of a subsidiary or division and shareholders wishing to sell a private company eventually should continuously be looking five years ahead.

Owners of private companies must realise that some will take five years from wishing to sell the company to the completion of the earn-out period following the acquisition. Listed companies should expect to receive payment in full on legal completion in the great majority of cases. It is still important to look five years ahead, because listed companies have a demonstrable tendency to procrastinate over selling a business which is non-core or only partly so.

Scarcity or rarity value is something that listed groups and owners of private companies alike should be ready to capitalise on. In these circumstances, it may be possible to realise a price for the business which is quite disproportionate to past, current or likely profitability of the business under present ownership, or the current value of the net tangible assets. It has to be realised that scarcity or rarity value is usually quite short-lived, and acquisition activity in a sector may well be followed by a period of rationalisation.

Profitability in the sector may decline, so acquisition prices will probably decline and businesses may even become unsaleable. A spectacular example was the UK estate agency market in the late 1980s. Major insurance companies and building societies set out to create nationwide chains of estate agencies. Almost frenzied acquisition activity led to excessive prices being paid, and by the mid-1990s it had become difficult to sell estate agency chains other than at a nominal price.

The timing of the sale process relative to the financial year-end of the company to be sold is worthy of consideration. If Heads of Agreement are being negotiated with about three months of the financial year remaining, the vendors should feel confident enough to warrant profits for the current financial year. If the vendors wait until the audited results are available, which would be at least three months after the financial year-end, they are unlikely to realise a higher price for the business.

Purchasers are likely to discount totally the budgeted performance for the financial year which has just commenced on the grounds that only two months of management accounts are available at that time. So by negotiating a deal towards the end of the financial year, it should be possible to obtain the same price for the business six months earlier than by waiting to present audited accounts to a purchaser.

## 2.4 Obstacles to selling

There are certain situations which deter prospective purchasers from acquiring the company until these have been resolved. Consequently, these issues need to be resolved before a business is offered for sale. It would be naive to think that a purchaser will not discover one of these problems during the due diligence carried out prior to legal completion. If this were to happen, the vendors would have incurred significant professional costs abortively and worse still it may be rumoured both within the company and in the marketplace that the business is being sold.

Likely barriers to a sale include:

- tax problems;
- litigation;
- compliance requirements;
- planning uncertainties concerning land and property;
- liability and warranty claims;
- legislation affecting product specifications and manufacturing processes.

It is not merely the reality of these circumstances which will deter prospective purchasers. The likelihood, threat or even possibility is usually at least as great a deterrent, because the uncertainty and delay are even greater. Each of these potential barriers will be considered in turn.

### 2.4.1 Tax problems

A routine investigation by the tax authorities into something seemingly harmless such as the payment of income tax and national insurance for employees should not be underestimated. Once a tax investigation is under way, the scope may become extensive. Consequently, any tax investigation, or notice that one is to take place, may cause prospective purchasers to withdraw. It should not be assumed that as the vendors will have to give comprehensive warranties and indemnities regarding taxation, a purchaser will view this as an adequate safeguard. At best, any purchaser is likely to insist on purchasing the business and assets only in these circumstances rather than the share capital of the company. This will almost certainly result in the shareholders of a private company paying more tax.

Prospective purchasers are right to be wary of potential tax problems. Significant professional costs are likely to be necessary and investigations are time-consuming for management.

Serious tax irregularities may arise as a result of the treatment of benefits in kind for directors and staff, and allowing people to be paid on a self-employed basis when they should have been taxed as employees.

### 2.4.2 Litigation

Litigation which could significantly affect the sales potential of a business will almost certainly destroy the prospects for a sale until it is resolved. One company which had established a worthwhile level of business in the United States received a letter from a major US company claiming an infringement of patents, which would be vigorously pursued. This claim was totally unexpected, considered to be of doubtful validity, but unfortunately was received just as the business was to be sold. A dispute of this kind may take years to resolve, and compensation claims and legal costs in the United States tend to be exorbitantly expensive.

### 2.4.3 Compliance requirements

Legislation is sometimes introduced which means that companies in a particular market sector will need to come under the control of a regulatory body by a given date, while failure to do so will prevent the business from trading. If there is a doubt about the capability of a company to meet the regulatory requirements, or significant changes and additional costs will be involved, this could affect the saleability and the price to be obtained.

### 2.4.4 Planning uncertainties concerning land and property

Planning uncertainties concerning land and building can be either positive or negative. Unfortunately, positive factors are unlikely to increase the realisable value for the business, but negative ones could make a business unsaleable until they are resolved.

A business may be located on a large site suitable for a supermarket or other sizeable retail outlet. Alternatively, the land might be attractively located for residential development. It has to be recognised that purchasers rarely increase their offer for a business to reflect the possibility of site redevelopment at some future date. Faced with this situation, if vendors wish to avoid giving away this potential benefit it is necessary to extract the freehold tax effectively from the company and to offer a medium-term lease to the prospective purchaser.

On the other hand, negative uncertainty such as the possibility that there could be a compulsory purchase order placed on part of a site for a road-widening scheme could be a deterrent to prospective purchasers. Worse still, road-widening schemes and urban bypasses may remain in the planning stage for several years before they are either implemented, changed as a result of local objections, or simply not proceeded with.

### 2.4.5 Liability and warranty claims

Environmental damage, land contamination or possible adverse effects on the health of staff, customers or the public at large are serious matters. Even if there is no indication whatsoever of any litigation being initiated, a prospective purchaser may either be intimidated at the prospect of a huge liability or will seek warranties and indemnities from the vendors of such a magnitude as to make the sale of the business unacceptable.

Serious design or manufacturing faults arising from the recent introduction of a new product are less daunting to a prospective purchaser. It should be possible for the purchaser to estimate fairly accurately the anticipated warranty costs in excess of the provisions already made in the accounts of the business, and presumably the vendors will be able to demonstrate unequivocally that the problem has been overcome.

### 2.4.6 Legislation affecting product specifications and manufacturing processes

European Union legislation is likely to continue to affect product specifications in various market sectors, not least in food products. Some legislation has meant that businesses have not only had to change the specification of their products, but production processes have had to be modified by a given date and this requires substantial capital investment. Prospective purchasers will reduce their valuation of a business in order to take into account the capital investment and product costs needed to meet future legislation. If they sense that a private company is unable to finance the costs involved, offers received for the business may be even lower.

### 2.5 Preparatory work prior to sale

An important issue to be decided at an early stage is what should be included in the sale. Specific issues include:

- avoidance of conflicts of interest;
- property ownership;
- overseas operations;
- central services;
- pension fund;
- company name;
- good housekeeping;
- maximising shareholder value.

Each will be considered in turn.

## 2.5.1 Avoidance of conflicts of interest

The purchaser of a private company will need to be satisfied that there will be no conflict of interest with the shareholders after the sale. Restrictive covenants will be imposed on the shareholders to prevent them competing for a limited period against the business they have sold, but there may be other complications. For example, the shareholders may own another business which trades with the business being sold. In these circumstances, it is unlikely that a purchaser would buy only one business because future profitability would depend on maintaining the trading relationship with the other business. Usually purchasers would insist on buying both the businesses, and there is a strong case for deciding at the outset to sell both if necessary.

Another possibility is that the shareholders own another business with a similar trading name which could cause confusion among customers. A purchaser may insist on purchasing both businesses or the vendors changing the name of their other business. When deciding what to include in the sale, the vendors must avoid any potential conflict of interest after the disposal.

## 2.5.2 Property ownership

The freehold property used by a private company may be owned by individual shareholders as a deliberate part of their tax planning. If the company and the freehold are owned by the same people, there may be no formal lease arrangement even though a commercial rent is paid for the use of the property. A decision should be made whether or not to include the property with the sale of the business; if it is not, a formal lease arrangement should be prepared.

Acquirers are right to be cautious when a company includes freehold property located overseas. Satisfactory evidence must be available to demonstrate the company has good title to the freehold, and any mortgage or charges against the property have been disclosed. If this is not the case, a prospective purchaser may insist on the overseas property being extracted from the company and a suitable lease being offered. At the very least, there could be a lengthy delay while investigations into overseas freeholds are completed satisfactorily.

The premises may be owned by a group property company. For simplicity, there may be neither formal agreement nor actual payment of rent, but merely a notional charge made for management accounting purposes. A decision must be taken either to sell the premises with the business or to offer a leasehold agreement. A possible complication arises when the business to be sold shares premises with another subsidiary, which is to be retained. The way in which the space is used may make it extremely difficult to separate the two businesses effectively on one site, and it may be necessary to sell the business on the basis of relocating it within an agreed period, assuming that the residual space can be used effectively.

### 2.5.3 Overseas operations

Some businesses, within a listed group or privately owned, may have formed companies overseas to protect the use of the company name. It is possible that these are either dormant or have never traded. None the less, any purchaser is likely to insist on acquiring these companies in order to maintain the protection of the company name.

Sometimes subsidiary companies trade overseas using sales or branch offices which are part of an overseas subsidiary of the same group. Consequently, staff located overseas may be employed by a local subsidiary. In these circumstances it will be necessary to transfer the employment of overseas staff to the company being sold, and to make appropriate arrangements for the continued use of space overseas in premises owned by a different group subsidiary. It may take several months to make a subsidiary or division into a saleable, stand-alone business.

### 2.5.4 Central services

Most subsidiary companies use some of the central services. Some of these are easily and quickly transferable when a business is sold – payroll preparation and pension administration may fall into this category. Dependence on an integrated information technology capability or network can prove difficult, because the acquirer finds that the hardware or software is not compatible.

It is usually inappropriate to remove this independence before commencing the sale process. Part of the detailed negotiations with a prospective purchaser should include agreement on a reasonable period for continuing to use the existing facilities on an agreed basis of charges.

### 2.5.5 Pension fund

The transfer of pension fund arrangements is a complex and lengthy process. It is likely that the staff being transferred on the sale of a subsidiary will be members of a group pension scheme. One alternative is to assess the pension fund liabilities relating to the business being transferred and to allocate an appropriate part of the group pension fund to meet the liabilities. Groups are understandably reluctant to transfer any part of a pension fund surplus when selling a subsidiary. If agreement cannot be reached on the amount of the fund to be transferred, another possibility is to leave the assets and liabilities with the vendor group and make future pension arrangements under the acquirer's scheme.

### 2.5.6 Company name

The name of many subsidiaries includes the group name. The vendor group is likely to insist that the use of the group name is discontinued either immediately on legal completion or within an agreed period, to avoid confusion. Also, the subsidiary may use certain patents, brand names, trademarks, copyright or other intellectual property which is owned by the group, and will continue to be used by other group subsidiaries after the sale. In these circumstances, some form of renewable licence agreement will need to be established.

### 2.5.7 Good housekeeping

The lack of what may be summed up as good housekeeping in some private companies may delay the legal completion of a sale. Any deficiencies should be corrected before initiating a sale. Furthermore, a demonstration of good housekeeping is often interpreted as a sign of professional management, which is reassuring to prospective purchasers.

Purchasers usually insist on acquiring 100 per cent of the equity at legal completion, and this applies to earn-out deals as well, even though some of the purchase consideration is deferred and dependent on future profit performance during a given period. Purchasers will want an assurance that all shareholders are prepared to sell in order to ensure that a disagreement among shareholders does not emerge after considerable management time and professional costs have been incurred.

The situation could be complicated when a financial institution is a shareholder. It is not sufficient to obtain an agreement to sell the shareholding because financial institutions may not be prepared to sell at the best price available. So it is essential to obtain agreement on the minimum acceptable purchase price. The situation can become even more complicated when several financial institutions are shareholders, which is often the case resulting from a management buy-out. It is essential that the lead institutional investor gives an assurance that a minimum acceptable price has been agreed. The opportunity to achieve a sale can be lost solely by an institutional shareholder refusing to accept a price which the individual shareholders found attractive.

Different classes of ordinary shares in a private company, with somewhat different rights attached, can frustrate the sale. Any sensible purchaser will simply offer a lump sum for the share capital of the company, and leave the shareholders to agree on the values to be attributed to different classes of shares. Unfortunately, attractive deals have been lost by the failure of shareholders to agree on the relative values of different classes of shares.

It would be wrong to recommend that the share structure is simplified before initiating the sale process, because legal costs will be incurred without necessarily adding value to either the shareholders or a prospective purchaser. It makes sense for the shareholders to agree on the relative value for different classes of shares before selling and to reassure prospective purchasers that disagreement among shareholders will not arise.

Although purchasers will insist on the protection of comprehensive warranties and tax indemnities in the legal agreement, they rightly draw considerable comfort when all taxation matters are in good order, up to date, and approval has been obtained for computations submitted to the tax authorities to establish outstanding tax liabilities. As soon as the possibility of a sale is to be considered, strenuous efforts should be made to bring the tax affairs up to date.

There is no advantage to be gained by choosing accounting policies which will inflate profits artificially. This will simply incur higher corporation tax liabilities than necessary and will not fool any prospective purchaser into paying a higher price for the business. When valuing a business, purchasers invariably recalculate the actual and forecast profits of target companies using group accounting policies.

Legislation in many countries requires that every employee, including shareholder directors, has a written contract of employment. Some private companies do not comply with this obligation, and this situation should be corrected prior to sale. It would be completely inappropriate, however, to seek protection for executives and staff by amending contracts of employment to give them extended notice periods prior to the sale of the company. This could either deter prospective purchasers or cause them to reduce the valuation to reflect the additional liability they would assume.

The lack of a formal budget and monthly management accounts makes a business less attractive to purchasers. Better still, there should be updated year-end profit forecasts produced on a quarterly basis to reflect the likely outcome for the current financial year as accurately as possible. Without budgets and monthly management accounts, many purchasers would not wish to value the business until the next set of annual accounts is available from the auditors.

Sometimes, numerous employees have individually negotiated incentive or bonus agreements based on quite different criteria. A purchaser may insist that any unacceptable incentive schemes are 'bought out' prior to legal completion by payment of a lump sum to each individual in return for accepting existing group incentive schemes. The purchaser may insist that the cost of buying out these incentive schemes is deducted from the agreed purchase price.

Intellectual property such as patents may be a valuable asset in some companies. Consequently, the administration needs to be in order and up to date. Patent renewal deadlines should have been met so that adequate protection exists. Furthermore, patents should have been applied for, not only in overseas countries where trading already takes place, but in those where potential for worthwhile future business exists.

### 2.5.8 Maximising shareholder value

Without doubt, the most important preparatory work to be done prior to sale is that designed to maximise shareholder value on the sale of the business. It is not something that can be done quickly; ideally it should commence up to two years before initiating a sale.

Many private companies prepare their accounts conservatively in order to minimise the corporation tax payable. This can be shortsighted in the period prior to a sale. Excessive provisions may be made against stock and work in progress valuations and other items designed to minimise taxable profits. A simple example will illustrate the potential loss of benefit to shareholders resulting from excessive provisions charged to the profit and loss account.

Assume that stock and work in progress are undervalued on the balance sheet at the time of the sale by, say, £150,000. Even though this may be pointed out to the purchaser prior to the valuation of the business, it is likely to have little or no impact on the price offered. Purchasers tend to look on any excessive provisions merely as offering some protection to offset any unexpected problems which may occur after the purchase has been completed. If the provision of £150,000 were released to the profit and loss account in equal amounts in the previous financial year and the year of sale, it would have a significant impact on the likely valuation of the business. By releasing the provision in this way, annual pre-tax profit would be increased by £75,000, which would be equivalent to an additional £50,000 allowing for the full rate of corporation tax. If the purchaser were valuing the business on, say, ten times the profit after tax this would increase the value of the business by £500,000.

If the sale is likely to include an earn-out arrangement, there could be a case for releasing the provision equally over the previous financial year, the current one and the year after the sale is completed. Otherwise, there is a danger that the profit thresholds to earn additional deferred consideration will be based on profit figures which are not sustainable. Consequently, earn-out payments could be reduced.

If the business is over-staffed, or there are people who should be dismissed or offered early retirement, action should be taken well in advance of initiating the sale so that the benefit is reflected in the profit and loss account. Otherwise, the purchaser will do this and enjoy improved profitability without any benefit to the vendors.

If, as a result of low inflation rates, an actuarial review of the pension fund shows that the level of company contributions can be reduced, at least temporarily, then the opportunity to increase profits in this way should be taken.

Before initiating a sale of the business, a recent revaluation of properties should be available. It is not necessary at this stage to pay for a formal revaluation, because a less thorough and brief written valuation may be sufficient. If the site has potential for residential or retail development in due course, the probability and likely timing need to be considered.

Ideally, a business to be sold will have demonstrated reasonable sales and profit performance during the previous three years compared with other companies in the same market sector. Some vendors wrongly imagine that because purchasers are acquiring the business to realise the future potential, the past is irrelevant to the valuation. This is simply not the case. Purchasers are rightly sceptical of vendors claiming that future profit growth will be spectacular despite an unsatisfactory performance during the previous three years. The forecast profit for the current year should reflect an improvement on the previous one in order to convince prospective purchasers of the likelihood of profit growth in the years ahead.

There should be demonstrable potential and plans in hand to grow profits throughout the medium term as a result of business development projects such as new products in the pipeline, branch openings, additional distribution channels or overseas expansion to be pursued. So it is important to achieve a balance between maximising profit prior to the sale and ensuring there is sufficient business development activity to ensure profit growth during the following two or three years. This is particularly appropriate when an earn-out deal is likely to be involved.

Purchasers usually 'add back' excessive pension contributions made by the shareholders of a private company when valuing the business. As more weight tends to be given in valuations to the level of profits, rather than the level of tangible net asset backing, there is a strong case for the shareholders making substantial lump sum contributions to a personal pension scheme in the two or three years prior to sale. As always, however, a balance must be struck. If the asset backing is over-depleted as a result of pension contributions, it is likely that this will reduce the initial purchase consideration to some degree.

When a business is auctioned, as is often the case with a government privatisation, a comprehensive Memorandum for Sale is essential. There may be 25 or more prospective purchasers wishing to make an offer for the business. It would be unthinkable for each prospective purchaser to be allowed to visit the premises and meet the management team. The Memorandum for Sale must provide sufficient information to enable prospective purchasers to make a meaningful outline written offer, subject to contract, based on the document alone.

The Memorandum for Sale is usually written by the advisers to the vendors, although it needs to be based on information and forecasts supplied to them by the management team of the business. Otherwise, there is a risk that the management may disown any forecasts, causing prospective purchasers either to withdraw their offers or to reduce them.

Typically, a Memorandum for Sale will include:

- an executive summary to give an overview;
- the history, ownership and current business;
- an assessment of the market segments and countries served;
- a description of products and services, with a comparative assessment of competitors;
- manufacturing processes and key sources of supply;
- major customers and distribution channels;
- freehold and leasehold premises;
- management, staff and organisation chart;
- intellectual property;
- financial information.

It must be recognised that a Memorandum for Sale should emphasise the future potential of the business to prospective purchasers. In addition to a forecast of profit and cashflow for the current financial year, future projections should be given even if only in outline.

When a business is to be sold by a direct approach to a shortlist of prospective purchasers, a Memorandum for Sale is not necessary. None the less, it is usual to prepare a business profile to be given to prospective purchasers after a confidentiality agreement has been signed.

About 10–15 pages of narrative, plus outline financial information and product or corporate brochures are adequate. The emphasis must be on selling the future benefits and opportunities to be gained by prospective purchasers. It should not divulge any commercially sensitive information, should avoid stating that the business is to be sold and not give an indication of the minimum purchase price required. If an acceptable purchase price is given, this is interpreted by prospective purchasers as the maximum price expected and offers are likely to be pitched at a lower level.

The benefit of presenting a business profile to a shortlist of prospective purchasers is to avoid a time-consuming and conspicuous site visit, which results in a prospective purchaser withdrawing as a result of obtaining information which should have been made available in the business profile prior to any visit.

## 2.6 Key point summary

1. Listed groups and shareholders of a private company should continuously look five years ahead to assess disposal.
2. Valid reasons for selling a business should not be ignored; a lengthy delay could significantly reduce the realisable value or make it unsaleable in extreme cases.
3. There are several different exit routes to selling a business to a trade buyer, and these should be evaluated at the outset.
4. Obstacles which are likely to deter prospective purchasers must be identified and resolved before commencing the sale process.
5. Scarcity or rarity value, which is often short-lived, may offer an opportunity to achieve a premium price for a business.
6. In the two years prior to sale, action should be taken to ensure that profits are fully stated to maximise the purchase price achievable.

# 3 Finding relevant businesses to acquire

Many companies find the most difficult part of making acquisitions is to open a dialogue with relevant businesses.

An Acquisition Profile, as described in Chapter 1, is the essential starting point. Otherwise wasted management time and unnecessary delay are likely. Even with the benefit of an Acquisition Profile, many acquisitive companies search for relevant business to acquire in a passive and unstructured way.

It would be myopic to restrict the search to those businesses which are known to be for sale. Many of the most successful acquisitions have resulted from a direct approach to businesses which were not for sale until the acquirer persuaded either the private shareholders or the group to explore the possibility of selling the business.

The first stage of an acquisition search needs to convert an Acquisition Profile into a 'shopping list' of relevant target companies, regardless of whether or not they are for sale. This is simply a process of identification. As the resulting list is likely to be too long to be manageable, an initial screening process is needed to categorise companies as:

- recommended acquisition targets; or
- borderline companies to be held in reserve; or
- rejected ones.

If the acquisition search is to be made in an existing market segment and a familiar country, it is possible that all the companies that fit the Acquisition Profile may be known to the acquirer. None the less, this should not be taken for granted. If the acquirer is planning to diversify, even into an adjacent market segment, it is unlikely that all the relevant companies will be known. Many successful private companies deliberately shun publicity and media coverage in order to avoid being pestered by potential acquirers. Yet it is these companies that can provide some of the most attractive acquisition targets.

It must be acknowledged that some private companies and groups will unequivocally reject any approach made by an acquirer. None the less, situations change. The death of a key director or significant shareholder in a private business may cause a change of mind. Equally, a different strategic focus adopted by a listed group may result in a business becoming non-core and a candidate for disposal. Consequently, even if an approach is rejected, it is important to confirm in writing that should the situation change, the company will still be interested in exploring the possibility of acquiring the business.

Analysis and serendipity do not produce acquisition opportunities. The experience of a subsidiary of a major listed group illustrates this well. About twelve relevant acquisition targets had been identified as part of a diversification strategy. Comprehensive information collection and analysis were carried out on each target company over a three-year period. The subsidiary was so determined not to reveal the plans for diversification that the acquisition requirements were not disclosed to any professional adviser or intermediary. Furthermore, they did not make a single direct approach to a target company.

In the meantime, three companies were purchased at prices lower than the subsidiary would have been prepared to pay for them. Naively it was imagined that prospective vendors would approach them, presumably as a result of some mystical process or telepathy. Given that the diversification plans were so clandestine, this was impossible.

The message should be clear. An effective acquisition search requires a systematic approach involving different avenues of approach as appropriate. Each of the main avenues will be described in turn.

## 3.1 Business for sale advertisements

In the United Kingdom, the *Financial Times* carries a considerable number of business for sale advertisements on Tuesdays, Fridays and Saturdays. In times of recession and during a lengthy recovery period, many of the advertisements are receivership opportunities. Private companies will be advertised for sale either under a box number or by a professional adviser on behalf of the vendors. Occasionally, a group will advertise the sale of a division or a subsidiary, almost certainly using a box number to avoid identifying the business to be sold.

The number of responses to a business for sale advertisement in the *Financial Times* is typically between 50 and 150. Clearly, neither the vendors nor any professional advisers can deal cost-effectively with every respondent. Their objective will be to find about six serious buyers, with a sound reason for buying the business and the ability to pay an attractive price. Replies from listed groups and substantial private companies are the favoured ones. Other private companies and management buy-in teams may be rejected with little or no consideration.

When replying to a box number, there is no second chance or right of appeal. Consequently, a private company responding to a business for sale advertisement should outline the reason for acquisition and demonstrate an ability to finance the acquisition, preferably without the need for raising additional equity capital. Also, there is a definite case for including the most recent annual report with the reply if this demonstrates an ability to finance the purchase. The aim must be to avoid rejection.

Vendors and their professional advisers tend not to give private companies the benefit of the doubt. They are unlikely to incur the modest expense of obtaining an annual report from Companies House. Even if they are prepared to consider a private company as a purchaser, they will probably request a copy of the annual report and evidence of the ability to finance the transaction. Rather than gamble, this information should be provided at the outset.

Management buy-in teams tend not to be taken seriously as prospective purchasers, even though this may not be in the best interests of the vendors. Consequently, a management buy-in team responding to a business for sale advertisement should include a brief description of their achievement in the same industry sector, an indication of the total amount of money the team is prepared to invest personally, and the name of a financial institution prepared in principle to finance them. Better still, a copy of a letter from a venture capital house expressing a willingness to back the management team to purchase a company up to a given amount should be included with the reply.

Advertisements placed by receivers demand an immediate reply. Receivers know that urgency is required if the business is to be sold as a going concern. At least 50 replies may be received by fax or return of post. Without waiting for further replies, they may decide which prospective purchasers they will deal with and despatch copies of the information memorandum immediately.

## 3.2 Disposal registers

A number of major accountancy firms maintain a disposal register of businesses for sale, and some of them network with other firms in order to offer the maximum number of potential acquisitions to prospective purchasers. These disposal registers typically include companies ranging from small ones to substantial businesses.

It is not necessary to be a client of the accountancy firm in order to access a disposal register. It should be realised that in view of the large number of companies which may be included in the register copies are not distributed to potential acquirers. Instead, the particular acquisition criteria of purchasers will be entered on a database and matched against available businesses.

Generally, no fee is charged for registering acquisition requirements. If the acquirer is an audit client of the accountancy firm, it may be possible to negotiate that no finder's fee is payable for an acquisition found from the auditors' own disposal register. If as a result of a networked disposal register an acquisition is made from the register of another accountancy firm, a finder's fee will be payable.

It should be established at the outset that a finder's fee is only payable on legal completion, and if either the purchaser or the vendor withdraw at any stage, there is no liability to pay the fee. It is important that acquirers using a disposal register recognise that in practice the level of finder's fees is demonstrably negotiable. The aim should be to pay only about 1 per cent of the gross purchase consideration of the business as a finder's fee.

## 3.3 Business brokers

It is commonplace for business brokers to work on a no deal, no fee basis. Therefore, any proposal that some fee should be payable must be firmly rejected. Business brokers usually do not work exclusively for a particular client. Some business brokers have been known to telephone prospective acquirers and offer them an acquisition opportunity on an exclusive basis but will only reveal the identity on pre-payment of a fee of several thousand pounds. Every acquirer should regard such practice as totally unacceptable.

Business brokers have a list of businesses which they are offering for sale, but not necessarily on an exclusive basis. In addition, some brokers will offer to carry out some speculative work at no cost in order to find relevant additional acquisition opportunities. It should be appreciated that it is unrealistic to expect a comprehensive search to be carried out without any guaranteed reward, and any businesses identified are likely to be offered to a number of purchasers simultaneously.

Most business brokers charge the acquirer, rather than the vendors. Before revealing the identity of any relevant businesses, the acquirer will be expected to sign a finder's fee agreement. Any small print must be checked to establish that a finder's fee is payable only in the event of legal completion. Some brokers' terms of agreement specify that the finder's fee is payable if either a written offer has been made, or if Heads of Agreement have been signed, whether or not the purchaser subsequently decides to legally complete the acquisition. Acquirers should reject such terms of business as unacceptable.

The standard fee scale used by most business brokers is:

      5 per cent of the first £500,000 of purchase consideration
*and*   4 per cent of the next £500,000 of purchase consideration
*and*   3 per cent of the next £500,000 of purchase consideration
*and*   2 per cent of the next £500,000 of purchase consideration
*and*   1 per cent of the balance.

This means that a finder's fee of £45,000 would be payable on a £1 million acquisition. In practice, finder's fees are negotiable and the benchmark should be 1 per cent of the gross purchase consideration. This should be regarded as fair reward for merely identifying an acquisition opportunity, as it is unusual for any business broker to provide any professional advice.

### 3.4 Corporate finance boutiques and merchant banks

It is a commonplace that there is hardly ever such a thing as a free lunch, but this may be one.

Whenever a corporate finance boutique or merchant bank is selling a private business or a group subsidiary the fee will be payable by the vendors. Furthermore, it is highly unusual for a corporate finance boutique or merchant bank to be involved in the sale of a business unless acting as exclusive advisers to the vendors. It would be an unacceptable conflict of interest if the boutique or bank were to seek or accept any finder's fee from the acquirer. Consequently, acquisitive companies should distribute their Acquisition Profile widely to corporate finance boutiques and merchant banks.

It is important to convince the boutique or bank that the prospective purchaser should be regarded as a serious buyer, rather than an opportunistic bargain hunter, with the finance available to complete an acquisition at a sensible price. Examples of recent acquisitions made, together with publicly available details of the prices paid, should be included to establish credibility as a serious buyer.

It must be recognised that any professional adviser acting exclusively on behalf of vendors will be seeking to offer the business simultaneously to a shortlist of about six companies known to be serious buyers. While the business is not being sold by a controlled auction, none the less a covert auction will be taking place, as shortlisted purchasers will be asked to submit an outline written offer, subject to contract and satisfactory due diligence, at roughly the same time. Based on these offers, and any subsequent clarification, a preferred purchaser will be selected for negotiations designed to reach Heads of Agreement.

### 3.5 Venture capitalists

Venture capitalists are a potentially fertile source of acquisition opportunities. The overwhelming majority of venture capitalists investing in a major buy-out or buy-in hope to realise their investment within 3–5 years or less, by the sale or flotation of the business. Only a minority of exits are achieved by flotation; the substantial majority take place by a sale to a trade buyer. While venture capitalists welcome opportunities to make an attractive exit at any time, they are understandably reluctant to acknowledge to a prospective acquirer that a business is for sale. On the other hand, they are prepared to be remarkably candid to corporate finance boutiques and merchant banks by identifying which businesses they would welcome receiving offers for, even though they do not wish to initiate a formal disposal process.

## 3.6 Business wanted advertisements

The use of a box number for a business wanted advertisement is likely to be an unthinking waste of money. Neither listed groups nor owners of private companies are likely to reveal a willingness to consider the sale of a business to the anonymity of a box number. The advertiser could be a direct competitor or a business broker looking for potential vendors while not acting on behalf of any particular purchaser. Either way, there can be no assurance of confidentiality. The willingness to sell the business may end up as widespread gossip, or even knowledge in the marketplace, with obvious damage.

None the less, business wanted advertisements placed by professional advisers can produce attractive acquisition opportunities. It is important that the advertisement is sufficiently specific to convince potential respondents that it is on behalf of a particular client, and not merely a catch-all to find vendors wishing to sell any business. Equally, the likely population of potential respondents should be assessed in order to be satisfied that a worthwhile number of replies will be received. Experience has shown that all the following components are necessary to produce a worthwhile response from a business wanted advertisement:

- the name of a reputable professional adviser in order to engender sufficient trust to persuade potential respondents to reply;
- the names of two individuals and a telephone number to persuade people to respond by telephone. The evidence is overwhelming that vendors have a marked reluctance to write in reply to any business wanted advertisement;
- an unequivocal undertaking that the identity of a respondent will not be revealed to the professional adviser's client without his express permission.

Results have demonstrated that the *Financial Times* is the most effective medium for business wanted advertisements in the United Kingdom. While the appropriate trade press may appear to offer a more focused and cost-effective avenue, the response may well be disappointing. One of the shortcomings is that acquirers do not read the trade press looking for acquisition opportunities because they do not expect to find them as business wanted advertisements are few and far between.

## 3.7 Comprehensive acquisition search

This is a time-consuming approach, but it is potentially the most effective one. Certainly, if the avenues described above have not delivered sufficient attractive opportunities, the only alternative is to carry out a comprehensive acquisition search in order to make acquisitions in a reasonable time.

The first step is to identify every company, subsidiary and division which appear to fit the criteria set out in the Acquisition Profile. The most effective way to ensure comprehensive coverage of a market sector is to use a combination of on-line databases, hard copy market sector surveys, trade association membership lists and personal contacts. This is likely to produce a long list of businesses which appear to fit the Acquisition Profile.

The next step should be to obtain the corporate brochure or product literature for each company in order to establish that it is not merely active in a market sector but that this represents the mainstream of the business. Where the acquisition search is aimed at a particular segment within a broader market sector, the only way to establish the relevance of the business is by examination of a corporate brochure or product literature. It will be necessary to ensure that the financial information is based on the latest annual report filed at Companies House, or an equivalent regulatory body overseas, and to obtain a complete copy of the annual report where appropriate.

One benefit of a comprehensive acquisition search in a market segment or sector is that it allows a useful picture of the sector to be compiled. Dominant players can be identified and assessed, even if these are obviously unsuitable acquisition targets, in order to understand driving forces and trends within the sector.

Corporate finance boutiques and the corporate finance departments of major accountancy firms offer a comprehensive acquisition search to clients. If it is relevant to obtain outside help, perhaps three prospective advisers should be beauty paraded. They should be questioned in some depth about the search methods they would use, and permission obtained to contact recent clients by telephone as referees. Unless the prospective adviser can undertake to carry out the search assignment exclusively for a particular client, without any current or subsequent conflict of interest, the adviser should be ruled out.

Any fee proposal based on the full cost of an acquisition search should be flatly rejected. There can never be a guarantee of success. Consequently, shared risk and reward are appropriate. The fee payable for a comprehensive acquisition search in a particular market sector in one country should be in the region of £5,000–£10,000, and this should include telephone contact with the decision-maker of target companies to initiate a discussion about a possible acquisition. An additional success fee of about 1 per cent of the gross purchase consideration payable on legal completion is fair reward for the work done. Reputable professional advisers will readily accept that they should make a loss rather than a profit on any search assignment, unless a legally completed deal results.

## 3.8 Overseas acquisition search

An effective acquisition search needs to be conducted with the help of people who live and work in the country.

Of course, it is possible to carry out a search programme from overseas by using sector surveys and on-line databases, which are available for most developed countries. There is no substitute, however, for effective personal contacts. These can include industrial gurus, recently retired executives, Trade Association Secretaries, venture capital houses, banks and the financial community generally. The evidence indicates that desk research is demonstrably not as effective.

In order to offer comprehensive acquisition searches overseas for clients, as well as in the UK, Livingstone Guarantee became active members of a network named Euro-Merger some years ago, which consists of leading corporate finance boutiques throughout Europe, Scandinavia, North America and beyond. It is worth repeating, there is no satisfactory substitute for local involvement in the search process.

## 3.9 Making contact

Attractive companies may receive at least one unsolicited letter seeking to acquire them every quarter. Not surprisingly, nearly every one is thrown in the wastepaper bin without reply. Some business brokers send out hundreds of these letters every week as a direct mailing exercise in order to find potential vendors. While their letter may imply that they are writing on behalf of a client, this may not be the case. When a willingness to sell is indicated, they will rapidly set out to find possible purchasers.

So, letter writing should be rejected. Fortunately, telephone contact works well. The crucial first step is to identify the correct person to telephone. Failure to get this right may destroy any chance of a positive response, because it smacks of a ham-fisted and unprofessional approach.

When wishing to acquire a subsidiary or division of a group, it may be tempting to telephone the managing director of the business concerned. It could be argued that one will need his or her support and co-operation in order to achieve post-acquisition success. The temptation must be rejected. It is quite possible that the approach will be thwarted at the outset either by 'forgetting' to notify the group, or mentioning it in a dismissive way, or worse still it may be a catalyst for the managing director to seek a management buy-out if there is a possibility the business may be sold.

The acquirer or professional adviser should identify the main board director who would make the decision whether or not a sale of the particular business might be considered, and telephone him. Prospective purchasers should recognise that groups tend to be utterly dispassionate when approached to buy a subsidiary or division, and will at least listen. In many cases, even if the business is not regarded as non-core, an opportunity to obtain an attractive price would be considered seriously. The group may request written confirmation of the wish to explore an acquisition from the prospective purchaser or the professional adviser before agreeing to an exploratory meeting.

When approaching a private company, it is often more difficult to identify the correct person to approach and to reach him. For example, it is possible that the principal shareholder has retired from the business and has given an instruction not to disclose a home telephone number.

It must never be assumed that the chairman or managing director is the correct person to approach in order to explore the possible sale of a private company. The person may be a salaried executive, and not a shareholder. The most recent annual report will reveal directors' shareholdings and identify the single largest individual shareholder; this is the person to contact. If the annual report reveals that one or more venture capitalists have an equity stake in the business, preliminary telephone contact should be made. The largest venture capital shareholder should be identified and a telephone call made to the executive currently responsible for the investment, who should be asked how the venture capital house would feel about a possible sale of the business, and how the individual shareholders may react. It should be pointed out that the telephone call is being made as a courtesy prior to making contact with the largest shareholder. In this way, useful information may be gained. Also, the venture capitalists will ensure that the matter is discussed with the shareholders in due course and not allowed to be rejected out of hand.

When a prospective purchaser telephones the largest shareholder in a private company, the objective of the call needs to be specific and limited. It could well be an invitation to lunch in order to discuss possible areas of mutual interest and co-operation. There is a danger that an outright request to explore the sale of the business will receive an immediate rejection as a reflex reaction without any consideration.

An alternative approach is to appoint a professional adviser, with a demonstrable track record of successfully approaching target companies, to make the initial telephone call. Curiously, vendors seem more receptive to a direct and explicit request from a professional adviser to explore a possible sale of the business. These telephone calls require thorough preparation and demonstrable expertise on the part of the professional adviser.

It must be agreed with the client before making a telephone call whether or not the identity of the prospective purchaser will be revealed. A willingness to reveal the identity of the prospective purchaser will enhance the chances of opening a dialogue. If this is unacceptable to the acquirer, the adviser will need to emphasise that the identity will be revealed at the outset of an exploratory meeting. In nearly every case there is much to gain and nothing to lose by revealing the identity of the prospective purchaser at the outset.

## 3.10  Key point summary

1. Notify corporate finance boutiques and relevant merchant banks of your acquisition requirements, because no finder's fee will be payable when they are acting as adviser to the vendors.
2. Insist that business brokers work on a no deal, no fee basis.
3. Regard finder's fees payable to business brokers and accountancy firms as highly negotiable, and ensure that a fee is only payable on legal completion.
4. Realise that vendors are unlikely to reply to a box number advertisement, so use the name of a professional adviser.
5. Recognise that local involvement is essential to carry out an effective overseas acquisition search.

# 4  Finding serious buyers

Ideally, every vendor would like to deal with only one prospective purchaser to obtain a legally completed sale at an attractive price. In this way, any damage caused by the possibility of a sale being leaked into the marketplace and fed back to employees would be avoided or minimised. Unfortunately, selling a business is not as simple as that, so everything possible must be done to maintain confidentiality.

Experience demonstrates that if at least four outline written offers are received for a business, the highest offer is likely to be at least 50 per cent more than the lowest one, and could be more than double in some cases. So every vendor faces a dilemma. Dealing with up to six known serious buyers is time-consuming and may increase the likelihood of a damaging breach of confidentiality. On the other hand, the result of dealing with only one prospective purchase may be that the offer is barely acceptable.

There is every likelihood that the acquirer will expect the Heads of Agreement to be signed within seven days of the final negotiation meeting, and to be accompanied by a binding exclusivity agreement prohibiting the vendors from dealing with other prospective purchasers until about 14 days after the planned date for legal completion. It is simply not possible to obtain alternative written offers within the seven days prior to accepting exclusivity. Knowing that experience shows that alternative offers vary widely in amount, the vendors may be tempted to reject the offer, only to discover in due course that the offer received was in fact the highest or even the only one forthcoming.

The approach should be to involve a shortlist of known serious buyers at the outset and to seek alternative written offers, before choosing the preferred purchaser and entering into final negotiations leading to the signing of Heads of Agreement.

## 4.1 Handling unsolicited approaches

Unsolicited approaches prove tempting to groups, private shareholders and venture capitalists if they are made effectively. An initial meeting may take place with the intention of simply satisfying curiosity or gaining market knowledge by learning about the acquisition intentions of a major player.

These are good enough reasons for agreeing to an exploratory discussion. A danger occurs when a professional adviser or prospective purchaser is sufficiently persuasive and persistent that the exploratory meeting leads to further discussions. At this point, the temptation can gather momentum, with harmful consequences.

Before proceeding beyond an exploratory meeting, conducted with caution, and having made it quite clear that the business is not for sale, the relevance of selling requires serious consideration. An assessment should be made as to whether or not the sale of the business is the preferred exit route, when would be the most relevant timing, how many serious buyers may exist and the likelihood of obtaining an attractive deal.

Major companies are as susceptible as private companies to have an exaggerated view of the saleability of a business and the likely price to be obtained. An informed second opinion should be obtained, without incurring any cost. It is perfectly reasonable to meet a corporate finance boutique, a merchant bank and the corporate finance department of an accountancy firm as prospective professional advisers. They should be asked to give an initial assessment of the probable deal which could be obtained, to identify a few likely purchasers and to outline the method they would recommend to achieve a legally completed deal. If professional advisers are unwilling to offer an initial opinion on valuation and likely buyers completely free of charge, and without any sense of obligation, they should be ruled out.

The only effective way to assess prospective advisers is to put them through their paces in this way. Before appointing any adviser, a further test should be applied. The deal leader should be asked for a binding assurance that he or she will be present at every meeting likely to involve any negotiation, and should be asked to supply telephone references of three clients for whom he has personally legally completed deals with recently.

The danger arising from drifting into a sale of the business as a result of an unsolicited approach is illustrated in the following example. A private company which manufactured and sold process control equipment received an unsolicited approach from the worldwide market leader. The managing director of the UK subsidiary company approached the principal shareholder and said he wished to merge the two businesses and was prepared to pay between £10 million and £15 million. By any stretch of the imagination, this was an unrealistically high figure.

The seduction continued. The case was made that as the proposal was to merge the two businesses, a thorough examination of the private company would need to be carried out in order to submit an investment recommendation to the overseas head office to justify a specific acquisition price within the £10 million to £15 million range. Over the next three months, a team of four from the prospective purchaser had open and intermittent access to the target company on site. No confidentiality agreement was signed, and an intimate insight of the business was given to the major competitor. Later, an outline written offer of £3.9 million was received from group headquarters. Not surprisingly this provoked anger, and an explanation was demanded as to why the offer had been reduced so dramatically. The reply summed up the naivety of the shareholders. They were told that the UK managing director had acted without the authority or even the knowledge of the head office.

The private company should have taken action to protect itself against a damaging and time-wasting episode. A simple request at the outset to confirm in writing the provisional £10–£15 million offer, subject to contract and due diligence, would have been sufficient. Directors of subsidiary companies in listed groups are not permitted to write such a letter without the approval of a main board director or group staff. Alternatively, by 'beauty parading' prospective professional advisers, as described earlier, a clear signal should have been obtained that the price suggested was nothing less than crude seduction and should be rejected or treated with extreme caution.

Unsolicited approaches may come directly from a prospective purchaser or via an intermediary. Both need to be dealt with effectively in order to avoid damage, gossip or even speculation. Any exploratory meeting with a prospective purchaser should not take place on the premises of the target company. Corporate life is incestuous. It is quite possible that a member of staff may recognise the prospective purchaser, as a result of working for that company or doing business with it on behalf of a previous employer, and this could lead to speculation that the business is being sold.

Even before agreeing to an initial meeting, a sensible question to ask is whether or not the person making the approach is acting with the knowledge and approval of the group. Before deciding to take matters further as a result of the initial meeting, the prospective purchaser should be asked to sign a confidentiality agreement. Also, the acquirer should be asked exactly what approval will be required before Heads of Agreement can be signed.

Some local subsidiaries, owned by an overseas group, are required to submit a detailed investment recommendation when Heads of Agreement are negotiated and before these are signed. At best, this could involve a delay of several weeks, and at worst the proposed acquisition may be rejected or an instruction given to make a reduced offer on a take it or leave it basis. To use a well-worn phrase, any prospective vendor must be satisfied at the outset that the director representing the prospective purchaser is a duly authorised 'organ grinder' and not merely an executive 'monkey'.

An unsolicited approach may be received by letter from an intermediary. The address may be quite revealing, indicating that the 'office' is merely the home address of a redundant executive who has decided to become a business broker. One option is to throw the letter away. Whatever the reputation and status of the intermediary or professional adviser, the specific identity of the prospective purchaser should be obtained, either prior to, or at the outset of, the meeting.

It is not enough to know the corporate name of the prospective purchaser; the individual executive's name, position and telephone number should be obtained. Some business brokers claim to be acting on behalf of a listed group when the reality is that the company is unaware that an approach has been made. The broker may have been invited to submit any relevant acquisition opportunities and has taken the liberty of using the name of the acquirer to justify the approach.

## 4.2 Fundamental issues

Many vendors, particularly private companies, are myopic when considering where potential buyers may be located. There is a tendency to assume that no overseas buyers will be interested in a relatively small company. This may not be true.

A packaging material distributor identified several major UK companies in the industry sector, received no serious interest at all and concluded that the business was unsaleable. The reality was totally different. Potential UK acquirers did not wish to make an acquisition because several major overseas manufacturers were intending to create their own distribution operation in the UK, so competition would intensify and profitability would be difficult to maintain.

Professional advisers were consulted and subsequently appointed. A shortlist of serious buyers was compiled of companies in Scandinavia, Europe and the United States. Five outline written offers were received and the business was bought by a major board manufacturer. Not only was the business eminently saleable, but a substantial premium price was paid to achieve the strategic benefit of obtaining a ready-made distribution network rather than creating one from scratch.

Many overseas groups when making a first acquisition in a particular country will only buy a sizeable business, which is operating profitability and has continuing management to offset the eventual departure of the founders or shareholders. Having made an initial acquisition in a country, there is often a willingness to acquire quite small businesses without particularly strong continuing management, because it is possible to integrate them with the existing business. So even businesses worth £1 million, or substantially less, could be attractive to major overseas companies. For example, a specialist refurbisher of passenger lifts was acquired by a worldwide manufacturer in order to acquire particular expertise which they did not have in that country. A small engineering consultancy specialising in underwater work was acquired by a worldwide group because they could exploit the demonstrable expertise internationally by cross-selling and so enhance the core business.

The only companies that become aware of the opportunity to buy a business should be those that are known to be serious buyers, committed to buying the particular type of business and capable of financing an acquisition at an acceptable price. It is not enough to work on the basis that the company appears to be a logical buyer, because a decision may have been made not to make any more acquisitions in the foreseeable future, or only to pursue opportunities which could result in a bargain price deal.

To establish that a company is a serious buyer it is necessary to identify the director responsible for acquisitions in the particular sector and country, and to ask explicitly the type and size of acquisition he or she is actively seeking. Obviously, a prospective purchaser is unlikely to reveal this information to a potential vendor, and equally the vendor would not wish to show his or her hand. None the less, major companies are usually willing to reveal their acquisition criteria to corporate finance boutiques and merchant banks in order to ensure that they are offered any relevant acquisition opportunities, in the knowledge that no finder's fee will be payable because the adviser will be working on behalf of the vendor.

Prostitution of a business must be avoided at all costs. Here some professional advisers are the worst offenders. It is totally unacceptable to work on the assumption that no damage will be done by offering a written profile of the business to prospective purchasers, provided that a confidentiality agreement is signed. Leaks do occur, despite the best intentions of companies acting with integrity. Occasionally they come about by deliberate intent. It should be obvious that if acquirers are asked whether they wish to receive the business profile of a relevant acquisition opportunity, they will almost certainly agree to sign a confidentiality agreement as a matter of course. Even if there is no interest in acquiring, it is an opportunity to gain information about a competitor.

In one case, professional advisers wrote to 118 companies inviting them to obtain a business profile provided a confidentiality agreement was signed. Over 100 copies of the business profile were despatched. Fortunately, some serious buyers emerged and the business was sold. The business had been grotesquely prostituted, and it was common knowledge throughout the market sector that the business was for sale.

## 4.3 Likely buyers

The purpose of the search should be to find about six serious buyers:

- with most to gain from the acquisition;
- able to finance a purchase at an acceptable level and to legally complete a purchase without undue delay;
- likely to develop the business and treat staff in an acceptable way.

Direct competitors in the same country may be the most dangerous prospective purchasers and the least likely to legally complete a deal at an acceptable price. They may pose as enthusiastic buyers in order to obtain valuable information about a competitor.

Relevant purchasers are likely to fall into the following categories, which are listed in a general order of attractiveness:

- Overseas companies in the same market sector, ideally having acquired another business in the country, but lacking a similar business to the target company locally.
- Companies already operating in the same market sector in the country but with a product or service gap. For example, a public relations consultancy may be particularly attractive to a media services group wishing to offer one-stop solutions to clients but presently lacking competence in public relations work.
- Groups operating in the same broad market sector and wishing to diversify. For example, a recruitment group specialising in financial appointments for banking institutions, commercial companies and the public sector may find the acquisition of a specialist information technology recruitment business to be relevant and attractive diversification.
- Companies which have fallen behind technological change. For example, electronic building management systems were largely developed, supplied and installed by newly formed private companies. Some major traditional control device manufacturers failed to respond to the business opportunity sufficiently quickly and the gap became too large to overcome other than by acquisition.
- Major customers or suppliers. It should be realised that many companies are reluctant to pursue vertical integration because this would result in competing with established customers. For example, a manufacturer supplying products through a network of wholesalers would be reluctant to acquire a wholesaling business, which would compete with existing customers. Equally, it should be recognised that few customers are prepared to pay an attractive price in order to acquire a supplier, because it would involve paying considerable goodwill for a customer base which may defect to other suppliers rather than buy from a competitor.

  None the less, if there is a lasting shortage of supply which could affect the growth of a major customer, an acquisition may be an appropriate means to protect a source of supply, though from the acquirer's standpoint, it may make sense to achieve a similar level of protection by acquiring only a minority equity stake.
- There is a surfeit of management buy-in teams seeking to buy businesses in many market sectors. Some of them will have a letter from a venture capital house expressing a willingness to be the lead investor to finance a purchase up to a given amount. It should be recognised that management buy-in teams cannot unlock the synergy which may be available to a trade buyer because they do not have any related businesses. Consequently, it may be difficult for venture capitalists to finance a purchase at

a comparable price to a trade buyer. Also, there may be problems or delays in syndicating the equity and debt finance required.

- Direct competitors should be regarded as possibly the least attractive of potential purchasers, and there may be sound commercial reasons why a particular competitor is regarded as an unacceptable acquirer. For example, it may be apparent that the competitor would relocate and integrate the target company with an existing business, causing substantial redundancies which the vendor would find unacceptable.

## 4.4 Avenues for search

The prime consideration must be to identify serious buyers without revealing prematurely the identity of the business to be sold. Avenues worth considering include:

- business for sale advertisements;
- personal contacts;
- disposal registers and business brokers;
- using professional advisers;
- a controlled auction.

Each will be considered in turn.

### 4.4.1 Business for sale advertisements

This is a safe way to identify prospective purchasers without revealing the identity of the business. Unlike business wanted advertisements described in Chapter 3, the use of box numbers is not a deterrent to prospective purchasers. The most effective medium for placing business for sale advertisements in the UK is the *Financial Times*. An advertisement will typically produce between 50 and 150 replies. Replies are likely to be received from individuals seeking a management buy-in opportunity, business brokers, professional advisers, private companies and listed groups or their subsidiaries.

The difficulty for the vendor is to establish which are replies from serious buyers, without revealing the identity of the business. Consequently, in order to avoid an exchange of letters using a box number, many vendors simply select listed groups or private companies known to be of a substantial size. Before revealing the identity of the business, a confidentiality letter should be signed by each prospective purchaser.

### 4.4.2 Personal contacts

These may provide some serious buyers. For example, any companies making an unsolicited approach to purchase the business during, say, the past two or three years may be contacted to find out whether they still have an interest in acquiring the business. Over the years, a number of potential relevant trade contacts will have been made at home and overseas. It may be appropriate to establish discreetly whether any of these are likely to be serious buyers.

If the company to be sold is a member of a trade association, the Secretary may be a useful source of possible buyers because some prospective purchasers make a point of letting the trade association Secretary know their acquisition criteria.

### 4.4.3 Disposal registers and business brokers

Disposal registers should be approached with considerable caution. By definition, any business that is listed on a disposal register is definitely for sale. Furthermore, it suggests that either the business is not sufficiently attractive and saleable to warrant a specific marketing campaign by professional advisers or, worse still, a marketing programme to sell the business has failed and it is now languishing on a disposal register in the hope that some unexpected buyer will emerge.

Some business brokers will undertake to contact prospective purchasers in addition to placing the business on a disposal register which is mailed widely to acquirers at large. When using a disposal register or a business broker, control must be exerted to maintain confidentiality. The intermediary should be given strict instructions that the identity of the company is neither to be revealed nor hinted at without the prior approval of the prospective purchaser by the vendor. Without this rigorous control, there is a danger of a damaging leak that the business is for sale.

### 4.4.4 Using professional advisers

There is a strong case for appointing professional advisers to carry out a systematic search internationally to produce a shortlist of known serious buyers. Relevant professional advisers include corporate finance boutiques, the corporate finance departments of major accountancy firms and merchant banks. During an exploratory meeting, the search methods used by the professional adviser should be established. Some rely simply on notifying overseas offices of the business to be sold, and passively rely on them to put names forward. A more systematic approach is required.

As prospective purchasers are likely to be sizeable companies, they are sufficiently visible to be identified from overseas. The professional adviser should be expected to use a combination of on-line databases and hard copy reference sources to identify prospective purchasers internationally. Then the decision-maker in each company should be identified and telephoned to establish what type and size of acquisition he or she is actively seeking in the particular country. Only in this way is it possible to produce a shortlist of known serious buyers, together with a reserve list of suitable companies and a brief reason for rejecting all of the other companies identified. Prospective purchasers seeking overseas acquisitions are generally eager to notify corporate finance boutiques and merchant banks of their acquisition criteria, knowing that when the adviser is acting on behalf of a relevant company there is an opportunity to be offered an acquisition opportunity without having to pay a finder's fee on legal completion.

When the vendors have agreed which prospective purchasers are suitable, the professional adviser should telephone the decision-maker and describe the business anonymously to confirm a definite interest to acquire. A confidentiality agreement should be sent and signed, before a profile describing the business is despatched. In this way, it should be possible to involve the shortlisted serious buyers simultaneously and to receive outline written offers in due course at about the same time, so that a preferred prospective purchaser may be chosen to negotiate Heads of Agreement.

### 4.4.5 A controlled auction

This takes the approach one step further, but it should be realised that it is only suitable in a minority of cases. The usual way to announce a controlled auction is by a press release to the leading financial newspapers in those countries where prospective purchasers may be found. Normally, the press release will specify the date by which outline written offers are to be received, and typically this is about four to six weeks after the announcement.

Suitable prospective purchasers will be given a detailed information memorandum after a confidentiality agreement has been signed and will be invited to submit an outline written offer without any contact with the management team of the business. From the initial offer letters received, up to six prospective purchasers will be invited to meet the management of the business and to confirm or amend their offer.

As a result of the second round of offers received, a preferred purchaser will be selected for detailed negotiation, and a second one should be kept in reserve in case of failure to agree a deal. While normally the purchaser will prepare the first draft of the Sale and Purchase Agreement, in a controlled auction the vendor may decide to prepare the first draft and is likely to distribute it to the shortlisted purchasers before resubmitting their offers.

Controlled auctions are widely used in the privatisation of businesses under public ownership. Where a listed group is selling a subsidiary and the likely purchasers are primarily direct competitors, a controlled auction may be appropriate. On the other hand, controlled auctions are rarely used for the sale of a private business because a covert auction as described earlier is more appropriate.

Before any decision is taken to hold a controlled auction, it is essential that the vendors are satisfied that the business is saleable at an acceptable price.

Otherwise there could be considerable embarrassment and the management of the business may regard the failure to sell as an opportunity to complete a management buy-out at a bargain price.

## 4.5 Key point summary

1. The aim should be to involve a shortlist of known serious buyers at the outset, and to obtain alternative written offers at about the same time.
2. The search for serious buyers needs to be international.
3. Direct competitors in the same country may be the least likely prospective purchasers to acquire the business at an attractive price, but appear to be the most enthusiastic ones.
4. Unsolicited approaches to acquire a business require a cautious response.
5. Controlled auctions are appropriate for the privatisation of businesses and occasionally for the sale of a subsidiary.

# 5 Initial investigation and due diligence

Some people confuse initial investigation and due diligence. Initial investigation should be carried out by a prospective purchaser when agreement has been reached with the vendors to submit an offer for the business. Even if a business profile describing the company has been given to a prospective purchaser, unless the sale process is a controlled auction, some supplementary information will be required in order to be able to value the business and to make a meaningful outline written offer. If a vendor demands that a written offer is submitted purely on the basis of a business profile, it should be realised that there is a risk that the purchaser will reduce or amend the offer, based on information received at a later stage.

Due diligence should not commence before Heads of Agreement have been signed. From the prospective purchaser's viewpoint, there is a risk of wasting money. For example, a major listed company spent over £100,000 on tax advice concerning the acquisition of a company in the USA, only to fail to reach agreement on the price to be paid.

From the vendor's standpoint, there is a strong case for insisting that due diligence work is not commenced on business premises until two working days after the draft Sale and Purchase Agreement has been received. In this way, the vendors have time to be assured by their solicitors that there are no unacceptably onerous clauses in the contract. This is an important safeguard for the vendors, because quite often staff realise that the business is being sold at an early stage in the due diligence process.

## 5.1 Exploratory meetings

At least one exploratory meeting should take place before the vendors agree to an initial investigation of the business by a prospective purchaser. In the case of an unsolicited approach, several meetings may take place over a number of months before the vendors are persuaded that an initial investigation should be carried out.

To avoid any speculation by staff that the business is being sold, exploratory meetings should not take place on the vendor's business premises. During exploratory meetings, the vendor should:

- obtain relevant information about the prospective purchaser, the method of making acquisitions and the approach to post-acquisition management;
- find out about any acquisitions the purchaser has made during the past three years, and what has happened to the businesses and the vendors subsequently;
- ask what plans the purchaser has to develop the company if it is acquired;
- outline the future potential of the business, underexploited opportunities to be developed and any benefits which are particularly relevant to the purchaser;
- avoid giving commercially sensitive information, such as terms of trade with major customers, process know-how, R & D projects and overseas sources of supply where no exclusive agreement exists.

Some purchasers fail to recognise the importance of first impressions created during exploratory meetings. Even when a business is unquestionably for sale, there is a selling job to be done by each prospective purchaser. From the outset, the aim must be to become the preferred purchaser in the minds of the vendors. The benefit of achieving this goes beyond the possibility of two purchasers making identical bids, and the vendors choosing a preferred purchaser on subjective grounds. It is quite possible for the vendors to choose a lower offer as the preferred purchaser because it is believed that a deal will legally complete at this figure, without undue delay.

The owners of a building products company received two offers – one of £6.5 million, the other £7 million – both payable in full on legal completion. The lower offer from a major UK listed company was accepted because the amount of due diligence work to be done was only about three days to be spent by two members of the acquirer's staff. In contrast, the US company which had made the higher offer planned to carry out due diligence over a four-week period involving a combination of UK investigating accountants and company executives from the USA. It was believed that the higher offer would eventually prove to be less than £6.5 million, because every excuse would be taken to find reasons for reducing the offer as a result of the extensive due diligence work to be carried out.

The most effective way for a prospective purchaser to persuade vendors to regard them as a preferred purchaser is to describe acquisitions already made. In this way, it is possible to outline the acquisition process already established, prices actually paid, deal structures and post-acquisition success. Better still, an invitation should be extended to telephone or meet vendors of businesses acquired to confirm what has been said.

Vendors of subsidiaries and private companies alike are concerned about what will happen to staff following the acquisition, so prospective purchasers should stress that either career opportunities and recruitment are envisaged, or at least existing jobs will be protected, if this is the case.

When an unsolicited approach is made, the vendors may say they are not prepared to sell the business for another two years, so that they can realise future profit growth from business developments already taking place. In these circumstances, it may be appropriate for prospective purchasers to suggest an earn-out deal whereby the vendors would be entitled to receive a substantial amount of deferred payment in order to benefit from the anticipated profit growth. If this approach is not sufficiently persuasive to create an acquisition opportunity immediately, it is important that the prospective purchaser should keep in touch with the vendors from time to time in case they change their mind about the timing of a sale.

Purchasers of private companies are rightly keen to ensure there is sufficient management continuity during the first two years after the acquisition is legally completed. Therefore, it is important that prospective purchasers find out the wishes of individual shareholder directors following the sale of the business and, if appropriate, make it clear that an earn-out deal involving some deferred purchase consideration would be a prerequisite. Equally, even at this early stage it is important to establish that the vendors do not have unexpectedly high price expectations. Understandably, the vendors may be reluctant to give any price expectation at this stage, but none the less the question should be asked. If no reply is forthcoming, prospective purchasers should give a broad indication of the likely purchase price to ensure that management time is not wasted on a deal which will never happen because of a fundamental disagreement over purchase price.

When agreement has been reached with the vendors to pursue a possible purchase to the next stage, it is important to discuss and agree on the extent of information to be exchanged before an outline written offer is made. The point must be made strongly to the vendors that more information must be made available if a meaningful outline written offer is to be made, and not merely a broad range of possible purchase price outlined.

Most prospective purchasers use less senior people to carry out the initial investigation than those used to make the high-level approach appropriate for exploratory meetings. Consequently, it must not be assumed that the scope and extent of information to be obtained during the initial investigation can be safely negotiated by the investigation team members when they start their work. The scope of the investigation needs to be negotiated by the high-level team used for the exploratory meetings, because they are well placed to deal with the vendors as equals.

## 5.2 Initial investigation

Except for controlled auctions when the outline written offer must be based solely on a detailed information memorandum, prospective purchasers must persuade the vendors to provide supplementary information before making an offer.

The purpose and scope of an initial investigation are not simply to verify past performance, or even the forecast profit for the current financial year, but to address future prospects during the medium term. An effective initial investigation should assess the gold ore still in the ground rather than counting the gold bars already in the vaults. This requires that the vital factors for future success in the business are identified and examined in some depth. While it is important to identify any vulnerabilities or negative features about the business, it is equally important to identify and assess profit opportunities and any undervalued assets.

There is inherently more risk in acquiring a private business than a subsidiary or a division of a listed group. Shareholder directors may have developed an eccentric style of management, and be unable to operate under the rigorous business planning, budgeting and management accounting procedures required by a listed group. In contrast, similar procedures are likely to be well established in a subsidiary or division and the existing management are likely to be keen to retain their jobs. On the other hand, the shareholder directors of a private company may be looking to leave the business as soon as possible or shortly after the end of any earn-out period.

## 5.3 Initial investigation team

There is the strongest possible case for carrying out the initial investigation using an in-house team, rather than investigating accountants or other professional advisers. Ideally, the investigation team should either be led by the person responsible for post-acquisition management or be accountable directly to him. In this way, accountability for post-acquisition success is established. The initial investigation provides an invaluable opportunity to gain first-hand knowledge of the business to ensure effective post-acquisition management. If the prospective purchaser is unable to assemble a suitably experienced team to carry out the initial investigation, there has to be serious doubt about the ability to manage the business effectively post-acquisition.

The investigation team should incorporate the different kinds of expertise which will be required for successful post-acquisition management. When acquiring a manufacturing business, the team should consist of a marketing/sales executive, a technical/operations executive and a finance manager. It is highly desirable that the team members have not merely had relevant operating experience at some point in their careers, but are still actively involved in an operating role. Otherwise, there is a danger that they are likely to be influenced by reminiscences based on their out-of-date experience.

While subcontracting the initial investigation completely should be rejected, the addition of one outside specialist to the team could be considered. This may be particularly appropriate if the team members have little or no acquisition investigation experience. In any event, an outside person could be used effectively to ask searching questions and to obtain sensitive information, so that the team leader does not compromise his or her rapport with the vendors.

One sensitive area which must be addressed in the case of a private company is the benefits enjoyed by shareholder directors. There may be an aeroplane or a boat owned and maintained by the company; members of directors' families may be provided with company cars. These items need to be identified, the costs involved estimated and reflected in the valuation. Those benefits that will cease immediately on legal completion must be pointed out to the vendors, tactfully but firmly, and an assurance given that the subsequent profit and cashflow improvement will be reflected in the offer to be made for the business.

## 5.4 Content of initial investigation

The investigation team need a checklist as a framework. If the acquirer does not already have an established checklist for initial investigation, the team should be asked to prepare one for approval before commencing work. In addition to general items which should appear on every initial investigation checklist, any key features relevant to the particular business or market sector should be added. For example, membership of an approved regulatory body may be necessary in order to carry on business.

Although the scope of the initial investigation should have been discussed and agreed at the exploratory meeting stage, vendors are somewhat surprised by the range and depth of information sought at this stage. Also, it is possible that the vendors need some time to compile information from the appropriate sources within the business.

It may make sense for the investigation team to have a brief preliminary meeting with the vendors, or at least a telephone discussion, to set out the information required in some detail. Some of this information may not be readily available, and the vendors may be reluctant to provide certain information at this stage even though it is available. If necessary, the investigation team should offer to collect or analyse information from files made available to them if the information is sufficiently important. When there is a reluctance to provide some information, selling, cajoling and negotiation may be needed. If necessary, the team used for the exploratory meetings should be asked to add their weight in order to secure important information.

During the brief preliminary discussion, the vendors should be asked to provide a copy of documents, such as the business plan, the annual budget and the latest set of monthly management accounts, so that these may be studied and relevant questions formulated. Also, the date, venue and length of time for the initial investigation should be agreed, ensuring that the vendors have been given sufficient time to prepare the information requested.

In most situations, the vendors will understandably be reluctant to allow more than a day for the initial investigation to take place, and should arrange a room in a nearby hotel in order to avoid undue speculation which might arise if the meeting takes place on business premises. It is important not to rely on anecdotal evidence alone when conducting the initial investigation. In a tactful way, the directors should be asked to support their opinions with appropriate documentary evidence.

In addition to the meeting designed to collect the information required for the initial investigation, it is desirable to suggest a brief follow-up visit or a telephone discussion about a week afterwards. This provides an opportunity to clarify any uncertainties and to ask any supplementary questions needed to complete the investigation work.

In many private companies, only the annual budget is available to make an assessment of future financial performance. It may be necessary to ask the vendors to prepare an outline sales and profit forecast for the next financial year, and to give some sales and profit projections for the following two years. The information and assumptions used by the vendors to prepare these forecasts and projections may be more important than the figures themselves.

These allow the investigation team to amend the underlying basis on which the forecasts and projections have been made, based on their own understanding of the business situation, and to prepare profit and cashflow forecasts on behalf of the acquirer. These should take into account any opportunities to be pursued and changes to be introduced under new ownership.

## 5.5 Scope of initial investigation

Some prospective purchasers restrict their initial investigation primarily to financial analysis. The scope of the investigation needs to be much wider in order to give an overall picture of the business, together with the vendor's view of competitors and the marketplace. The aim should be to carry out a wide-ranging assessment of the business and the marketplace, and to identify suspect features which will require an in-depth investigation at the due diligence stage once Heads of Agreement have been signed. The information needs to be adequate to make profit and cashflow projections in order to value the business. It is totally unacceptable merely to accept the figures put forward by the vendors. Equally, an assessment is needed of the current worth of the company assets, and any opportunities available either to sell surplus assets or to reduce the amount of working capital required.

The scope of the initial investigation should include:

- History of the company
  - date of formation and important events

- Share capital
  - authorised and issued
  - present ownership
  - significant past changes of shareholdings
  - relationship between shareholders
- Business
  - sales history
  - key customers, suppliers and contracts
  - pricing of products and services, compared with competitors
  - forward orders, and likely profitability of these
  - R & D projects
  - accounting policies
  - bad debt history and current provisions
  - stock and work in progress analysis
  - analysis of sales by distribution channels
  - vendor's assessment of competitors and market
- Land and buildings
  - location
  - freehold and leasehold details
  - amount of floor space
  - condition of property
  - most recent valuation of freeholds
  - terms of any space let
  - surplus space
  - planning status
  - planned improvements and potential for alternative use
  - insurance cover
  - estimated cost of refurbishment required by acquirer
- Plant and equipment
  - plant capacity and efficiency
  - balance sheet value by category
  - age and condition of major items
  - capital expenditure contracted, authorised and budgeted
- Mortgages, loans and overdraft
  - facilities available and used
  - conditions and terms
  - interest rates
- People
  - employee numbers by department
  - key staff
  - typical salaries, bonuses and fringe benefits
  - service contracts
  - share option schemes
  - pension fund

- health and safety matters
- compatibility of culture and style
- Contingent liabilities and issues
  - major litigation
  - excessive warranty claims
  - claims resulting from environmental damage
  - tax investigations in progress and pending
- Directors
  - shareholdings in other companies
  - other directorships
  - pensions payable to former directors
  - relatives employed
  - use of company boat or plane
  - corporate sponsorship
  - other benefits

## 5.6 Due diligence

Some acquirers naively think that due diligence is an optional extra because stringent warranties and indemnities will provide adequate protection. This could prove to be a false and costly economy – even a disastrous one. Whenever a private company is acquired, there is always the possibility that the shareholders will have either transferred their purchase consideration or spent it before warranty and indemnity claims are made. In any event, litigation is costly and a drain on management time.

Furthermore, when claiming against a breach of warranties the onus of proof is placed on the acquirer to establish that it has suffered loss as a result of the breach – in other words, to justify the amount by which the purchase price should have been reduced if the breach of warranties was known at the time of acquisition.

Due diligence is an essential and cost-effective protection, which should be carried out by every acquirer. The solicitors acting on behalf of the acquirer, whether in-house staff or a professional firm, should carry out the necessary legal due diligence. Matters affecting freehold property, leaseholds, material contracts, conditions applicable to outstanding liabilities, intellectual property such as patents and trademarks and any licensing or royalty agreements should be covered as a matter of course.

Financial and tax issues need to be investigated in depth. Unless the prospective purchaser has staff available with previous experience of this work, investigating accountants should be appointed. Most acquirers use the specialist investigation department of their auditors, provided the firm is sufficiently large to have one.

If there are reservations about using the auditors as investigating accountants, or the firm does not have a specialist department, then two or three major accounting firms should be beauty paraded. It is important to establish that the team carrying out the due diligence work has some experience of the particular market sector, or at least of a similar business. The insight gained from previous experience can be invaluable in revealing problems within the target company which might otherwise be missed.

Before appointing any firm of investigating accountants, the scope of the investigation, terms of reference and the maximum fee chargeable should be agreed. If the acquirer does not either specify or agree the terms of reference with the investigating accountants, there is a risk that they will carry out an unnecessarily wide-ranging investigation in order to maximise their fee income.

Some investigating accountants will carry out an assessment of the market sector in which the target company trades, unless instructed otherwise. Having signed Heads of Agreement, the acquirer should have completed an assessment of the market sector long ago. If not, it does not necessarily follow that the investigating accountants are best equipped to carry out this assessment. Failure to agree the terms of reference is likely to result in unnecessary due diligence expense.

## 5.7 Environmental issues

Environmental issues have become important to acquirers, and it may be necessary to appoint specialist environmental consultants to carry out the appropriate due diligence.

No buyer or seller should regard themselves as immune from environmental issues. Furthermore, legislation worldwide is becoming more onerous and enforcement stricter. History cannot be ignored. Buildings sited on reclaimed land, perhaps dredged from a polluted harbour bottom, and former landfill sites are obvious examples of environmental risk. Vendors may not regard contamination as a risk, but they could be a victim if the buyer withdraws as a result of carrying out environmental due diligence.

There should be written records of site usage wherever appropriate. The type of waste produced, the quantity and the ultimate method of disposal need to be documented. There must be a demonstrable record of prompt and full disclosure to staff and the local community whenever pollution or contamination could cause any risk to health, and timely action must be taken to correct matters. Formal consents, control orders and certificates for atmospheric emissions and liquid or solid waste disposal must be in place, and the appropriate procedures followed consistently. The permission granted needs to allow sufficient capacity to match the expected growth of the business throughout the medium term.

Where the vendors know that a site is contaminated there could be a case for having an environmental audit carried out so that a copy can be given to prospective purchasers at the outset. Otherwise, there is a risk that a deal will be agreed and Heads of Agreement signed, only to be subject to re-negotiation by the acquirer after environmental due diligence has been carried out and shortly before legal completion. In extreme cases, the deal could fail because the acquirer finds the environmental risk unacceptable.

## 5.8 Commercial due diligence

Commercial due diligence receives inadequate attention from many acquirers, including multinational companies which should certainly know better. There is a demonstrable willingness by acquirers to accept anecdotal evidence put forward informally by vendors as reliable information. Often little or no effort is made to verify these statements. Yet the prime cause for acquisitions proving to be significantly less successful than expected is an inaccurate assessment of commercial matters within the target company.

It is simply not acceptable to rely on assertions by the vendors that their products and services are the best in the market sector, and competitively priced as well. According to the type of product or service involved, the acquirer should purchase or use competitive products and services, or, if this would be prohibitively expensive, at least beauty parade competitive suppliers and listen to what they have to say. Vendors often claim that their products are generally accepted by customers or clients as the best available. This should be put to the test. It is possible to appoint specialist advisers to contact both customers and prospective customers using market research techniques to carry out a comparative analysis of the target company against other competitors.

The essence of due diligence is to identify every facet of the target company and the business environment which could have a significant effect on post-acquisition success, and to carry out affordable investigation work before legal completion. If the vendors are reluctant to co-operate or to give the access required for adequate investigation, they must be tactfully and formally reminded that legal completion is subject to a comprehensive due diligence programme being carried out, with acceptable findings.

## 5.9 Key point summary

1. Vendors should allow limited initial investigation of the business to ensure outline written offers are meaningful, unless the sale process is a controlled auction.
2. The initial investigation should be carried out by the acquirer's staff, led by or reporting to the person accountable for post-acquisition success.
3. Due diligence should not be commenced until Heads of Agreement have been signed.

4. Commercial and environmental due diligence are as important as financial, tax and legal matters.
5. Written terms of reference and a maximum fee should be established before advisers are appointed to carry out any due diligence work.

# 6 Valuation and deal structure

There is no such thing as a correct valuation of a private business or the subsidiary of a group. Indeed, it can be argued that the only accurate valuation is the highest amount which a purchaser is willing to pay for the business. The empirical evidence shows that when at least four outline written offers are received for a business, the highest one is likely to be more than 50 per cent greater than the lowest one. Occasionally, the highest offer received is more than double the lowest one.

## 6.1 Valuation issues

While rigorous financial analysis is the foundation for valuing a business, there are less tangible factors which both buyers and sellers should take into account.

Although the basis of any valuation should be the profit and cashflow projections for the current and future years, past results should not be ignored. There is greater comfort when acquiring a business which has achieved sales and profit growth during the past three years, which is consistent with future projections, compared with a business which has performed erratically in recent years, or is currently loss-making and the vendors claim that dramatic profit growth is about to be realised.

The sales and profit performance for the past three years should not be accepted at face value. The apparently steady growth in sales and profits may reveal results which have been bolstered by one-off events. For example, a temporary shortage of supply may have enabled a manufacturer to increase prices significantly for a while. Alternatively, the results of a previous year may include the benefit of a substantial order which represented a unique sales opportunity. Conversely, past results which indicate an erratic performance may simply be the result of one-off external events which have adversely affected performance. For example, a brochure printing company may have suffered a substantial bad debt as a result of the collapse of a major package holiday company.

If there is a lack of suitable acquisition targets in a particular market sector within a country, the rarity or scarcity value is likely to increase the price that prospective purchasers are prepared to pay. In these circumstances, it may be possible to achieve a purchase price which is disproportionately higher than either past, current or likely profitability and the current value of net tangible assets could justify. Vendors must realise, however, that rarity or scarcity is usually only a temporary opportunity.

Companies faced with a shortage of attractive target companies may decide to enter the market either by acquiring a smaller or less attractive company and investing heavily post-acquisition, or by starting a business in the country concerned. The result may be that prospective purchasers are no longer keen to make an acquisition, but instead have become established competitors. So not only has the opportunity to capitalise on rarity or scarcity value been lost, but the vendors are likely to face the prospect of increased competition as well.

Vendors should compare their assessment of the value obtainable by selling the business to a corporate buyer, with other available exit routes. For example, by waiting for another year or two the company may grow sufficiently to justify a stock market flotation.

If the business is presently making a loss, a valuation of the business today should be compared with the price likely to be achievable in about two years' time after the business has been returned to profit. Prospective purchasers should take into account the time and cost required to create a similar business from scratch, in order to gain further insight into the value of a target company to them.

For example, a company may have a strategic goal to build a nationwide chain of distribution outlets. In one particular region of the country a competitor may have achieved a dominant position. The length of time and cost required to create a similar business either from scratch, or by a combination of piecemeal acquisitions and the opening of new outlets may be significantly greater. Also, it should be recognised that while an increase in the number of distribution outlets is likely to increase the size of a market in that region, the result is likely to be a disproportionately larger increase in competition.

Both acquirers and vendors should quantify synergy, and any financial benefits resulting from the acquisition which would be accounted for elsewhere in the acquiring group. For example, the financial and commercial justification for insurance companies paying extravagant prices to acquire estate agency businesses was that they would make substantial additional profits in their endowment policy divisions by the sale of policies to estate agency customers. Every acquirer should realise that synergy is easier to calculate than it is to unlock post-acquisition.

It is unacceptable to justify a valuation which includes the realisation of post-acquisition synergy, on the assumption that when the business has been acquired ways will be identified to unlock the synergy. Before including synergy for acquisition valuation purposes, the method and costs of unlocking it need to have been formulated, at least in outline. Furthermore, to rely on untested hunches is equally unacceptable, attempts must be made to collect evidence to test the assumptions on which synergy has been calculated.

## 6.2  Adjusted profits and balance sheet worth

A key factor in the valuation of any business should be the projections of profit and cashflow which will be achieved by the purchaser. It must be recognised, however, that the profit and cashflow generated will be different under new ownership.

Although purchasers will pay particular attention to future profit and cashflow projections, it makes sense to restate the figures for the previous financial year to ensure a sound starting point. Whenever professional advisers are acting for vendors, they will usually restate the previous three years' results in order to demonstrate the true level of profits any purchaser would have enjoyed.

A purchaser should restate previous year's profit and loss accounts to reflect the way in which the business would have been managed by them. For example, relevant adjustments could include:

- the need to increase salaries to eliminate unacceptable differences compared with similar staff already employed within the group;
- the appointment of a qualified financial controller in addition to the existing accounting staff;
- the need to increase an inadequate level of professional indemnity cover;
- any additional pension costs if staff are to be invited to join the group pension scheme which will require higher contributions.

Both the purchaser and the vendor should identify and quantify opportunities for increasing profit and cashflow generation post-acquisition. Typically opportunities include:

- reduced purchase prices as a result of increased purchasing power;
- savings arising from the rationalisation and integration of premises, equipment and staff;
- cross-selling products and services of the acquired company to existing group customers in the territories already served, and vice versa;
- expanding overseas sales by distributing the products and services of the acquired company through existing group outlets.

Vendors and their professional advisers should restate current and previous year figures to reflect one-off events which have significantly reduced profits and costs and which will not necessarily be incurred after a change of ownership. These include:

- the cost of relocating premises;
- any industrial action affecting deliveries from a key supplier or limiting sales to a major customer;
- the cost of major litigation;
- the withdrawal of a product or the closure of an office or factory;
- redundancy costs;

- substantial pension contributions on behalf of directors;
- start-up costs connected with a new product launch or overseas expansion;
- a reduction of directors' salaries post-acquisition to reflect a fair reward for their executive role rather than the benefits of an owner;
- the retirement or departure of a director who will not need to be replaced;
- savings arising as a result of relatives leaving the business.

When selling a division or subsidiary, it is common practice among professional advisers to restate the profits by adding back any charges allocated to the business which would not be made following the disposal. Typically allocated costs include:

- a group management charge to reflect a portion of corporate head office costs;
- a percentage charge based on sales turnover or on assets employed to cover group expenditure on items such as research and development or advertising designed to promote the group as a whole;
- service charges reflecting the use by the business of central departments such as information technology, payroll and pension administration, and so on.

The justification for adding back allocated charges is that the acquiring company will be able to replace the benefits and services at a much lower incremental cost than the current allocated charges. The vendor group should recognise that, following the disposal of a subsidiary, it is rarely possible to reduce the actual costs to the same extent as the allocated charges made to the business which has been sold.

The most recent financial year-end balance sheet should be adjusted to reflect the current net asset value of the business by taking into account:

- the current market value of freehold premises;
- any surplus assets which the acquirer could realise in excess of the written down value;
- any understated current assets such as stock, work in progress and debtors.

Vendors should project the current net asset value of the business at the time of legal completion to take into account retained profits during the current year and any planned distributions such as dividend payments or substantial pension contributions for directors.

## 6.3 Cashflow projections

Vendors should recognise that different prospective purchasers may enjoy different benefits and opportunities as a result of acquiring a particular business, so an assessment of the synergy to be unlocked by each purchaser should be made where appropriate. Purchasers should make detailed cashflow projections, for at least the next three years, as the basis for using discounted cashflow analysis valuation techniques. In most market sectors cashflow projections beyond the next three years are largely guesswork and consequently a broad brush approach is appropriate. Items which need to be taken into account include:

- any cash balances in the company to be acquired;
- the need to repay, reduce or restructure existing loan and overdraft facilities;
- capital expenditure required to refurbish premises to meet group standards and to replace existing assets which are worn out;
- capital expenditure required to meet forthcoming or anticipated legislation which will affect operating methods or impose stricter environmental regulations;
- capital expenditure needed to overcome existing bottlenecks or to meet planned expansion;
- expenditure needed for compatibility of information technology systems and the need to improve management information;
- the amount of cash generated, or additional funds needed as a result of the planned business growth and development;
- cash generated from the sale of surplus assets.

If vendors do not carry out detailed cashflow projections covering the first three years post-acquisition, there is a danger that the value of the business may be underestimated. Equally, the projections must be based on what the particular acquirer can generate and not merely the cashflows which would have been achieved under present ownership. Vendors should pay particular attention to cash which could be generated by selling surplus assets or significantly reducing working capital, because this effectively reduces the purchase cost to the acquirer and should be reflected in the amount paid. Better still, these opportunities should have been realised by the vendors before initiating the sale process.

The majority of service businesses are sold on an earn-out deal basis, involving the opportunity to earn an additional payment based on the vendor's ability to increase profits during the first two or three years post-acquisition. Only by making cashflow projections can vendors assess the extent to which the deferred purchase consideration is to be paid out of cash generated by the business during the earn-out period. If this is the case, it should be taken into account in negotiating the initial payment because effectively the earn-out will be self-financing.

## 6.4 Valuation techniques

Rigorous calculations and projections of adjusted profits and cashflows, together with the current net asset value of the business at the time of legal completion, are the foundation for any valuation. It must always be remembered that no valuation technique can enhance the inherent accuracy or lack of it in the profit, cashflow and asset value projections. Equally, it would be entirely wrong to assume that an accurate valuation can be made simply by the application of valuation techniques, formulae and criteria. Much less quantifiable factors must be taken into account as these could have a significant impact on the realisable value of a business. For example:

- an acquisition of disproportionate strategic significance to an acquirer, perhaps an intention to enter a different market sector or country by acquisition to be followed by a major commitment to achieve rapid organic growth;
- a defensive need to acquire, because the acquirer has fallen behind technological developments within the market sector;
- the vendors face a cashflow crisis which could result in either receivership or breaching banking covenants.

The valuation techniques and criteria commonly used by acquirers and professional advisers are:

- return on investment;
- discounted cashflow analysis techniques;
- an earnings multiple valuation;
- net asset backing;
- impact on earnings per share for a listed company making a significant acquisition.

Any business valuation should be based on the use of at least two valuation techniques, because any one method tends to have an in-built bias. These techniques and criteria will be described in turn.

### 6.4.1 Return on investment

A simple method for valuing a business is to calculate the return on investment to be achieved by the acquirer. It is sufficiently simple that non-accountants are able to use this technique to produce reliable valuations. On the other hand, this method is equally popular with chief executives of listed groups as a means of cutting through the sophisticated financial analysis often carried out by the finance department.

Return on investment, often referred to as ROI, can be defined in various ways. For the purpose of business valuation a simple and relevant definition is:

$$\text{Percentage ROI} = \frac{\text{Pre-tax profit}}{\text{Net cash invested}}$$

Many listed companies seek to achieve a return of about 18–22 per cent based on this definition, but realise that the purchase price needed to acquire a business means that this target level of return will only be achieved during the second financial year following acquisition, and as a result of post-acquisition business development.

In the most simple case, consider a business acquired in 1995 which would achieve additional pre-tax profits for the acquirer of £1 million in 1997. If the acquirer is prepared to accept a return on investment of 20 per cent pre-tax in the second financial year following acquisition, the business would be valued at about £5 million, because a return of £1 million pre-tax profit on a £5 million net investment gives a projected return of 20 per cent.

A more typical example will be illustrated to take account of anticipated earn-out payments and cash generated in the business. Consider a specialist printing company purchased for £4.0 million and an anticipated earn-out payment of £0.5 million in the second year following acquisition. Cash generated within the business is projected by the acquirer to be £0.1 million in the current financial year, and £0.4 million and £0.5 million in subsequent years.

|  | Current year | First post-acquisition year | Second post-acquisition year |
|---|---|---|---|
| Pre-tax profit forecast | £600,00 | £650,00 | £700,00 |
| Purchase consideration | (£4.0m) | – | (£0.5m) |
| Net cash generated | £0.1m | £0.4m | £0.5m |
| Cumulative net cash invested | £3.9m | £3.5m | £3.5 |
| Return on investment equals | 600,00 | 650,00 | 700,00 |
|  | 3.9 | 3.5 | 3.5 |
|  | 15.4% | 18.6% | 20.0% |

From the standpoint of an acquirer, a return on investment target to be achieved by the second financial year following acquisition might be seen as taking too short-term an outlook. Some experienced corporate chief executives take the view that if synergy has not been unlocked by then, it may never happen, and forecasting the future three or more years ahead is notoriously inaccurate. Consequently, they are happy to acquire businesses which have demonstrable long-term strategic relevance for the group, and which deliver an acceptable return on investment in the medium term. Given stock market pressures for short-term performance in some countries, this is an understandable and reasonable outlook to take.

### 6.4.2 Discounted cashflow analysis

This technique is somewhat complicated to use, but is probably the most relevant business valuation technique.

Discounted cashflow techniques are widely used by listed groups to evaluate capital expenditure projects. Rather disappointingly some smaller and medium-sized listed companies still do not use these techniques for acquisition valuation.

It is generally recognised that the most relevant basis of valuation is to compare the cashflows generated by the investment and the timing of these flows in relation to the cash invested. This approach is the foundation of discounted cashflow analysis.

To assess the value of a business using discounted cashflow requires cashflows to be calculated over a period of several years. Particular attention should be given to cashflow projections for the first three years, because additional weight is given to cashflows generated in the early years after investment. Also, recognising the uncertainty and likely inaccuracy when forecasting cashflows more than three years forward, it is adequate to adopt a broad brush approach for later years.

For those unfamiliar with discounted cashflow analysis, only elements which affect cashflow are taken into account and these need to include:

- the initial purchase consideration;
- any subsequent earn-out payments;
- the operating cashflow from the business, taking into account both capital expenditure and working capital needs;
- the realisable value of the remaining assets at the end of the evaluation period, rather than a going concern valuation of the whole business;
- tax payments.

Once the net annual cashflows have been evaluated, these should be used to calculate the Net Present Value, the internal rate of return or the discounted pay back period.

Net Present Value (sometimes referred to as NPV) is the present value of the cashflows calculated at the percentage rate set by the company.

The internal rate of return is used more widely than NPV because managers more easily understand it. The projected percentage rate of return is calculated by identifying the percentage discount rate at which the NPV of the cash outflows and inflows equals zero over the evaluation period chosen. Alternatively, the pattern of cashflows can be modelled financially at the required percentage rate of return in order to calculate the maximum acceptable acquisition price.

The discounted payback period is the number of years required to generate sufficient cash at the present value to match the cash required to acquire the business. Those companies that calculate and use discounted payback periods for evaluation usually choose a standard rate for the weighted average cost of capital net of tax. It is calculated to take into account the mixture of equity finance, loans and overdraft, and the dividend or interest rate payable on each type of finance.

There is no doubt that discounted cashflow analysis is as relevant for business valuation purposes as for internal capital expenditure projections.

None the less, some companies encounter pitfalls in using these methods and it is important to avoid them.

When evaluating internal capital expenditure projections, only the realisable value of the assets remaining at the end of the evaluation period is taken into account. Similarly, no attempt should be made to take into account the terminal value of the acquisition on a going concern basis, or to value either the goodwill or intellectual property, in order to offer a meaningful comparison with internal investment projections. This is necessary for consistency and comparability. No attempt should be made to choose an evaluation period which equates to the expiry of the business opportunity. On the other hand, there is a strong case for a group insisting on standard periods of evaluation to be used for projections in order to ensure comparability.

Perhaps the most important benefit of using discounted cashflow techniques is the ease with which sensitivity analysis can be carried out to answer 'what if' questions. For example, there may be an identifiable risk of the acquired business losing a major customer or client because of a conflict of interest arising from group ownership. Once the basic cashflows have been calculated, it is easy to adjust them to reflect different assumptions about the extent and timing of business which might be lost by a conflict of interest, so that the impact on the NPV, percentage rate of return or discounted payback period can be calculated.

Provided that potential opportunities and vulnerabilities can be identified and the cashflow impact calculated, it is possible to determine how significant the effect will be on the return to be achieved. In this way, it is possible not only to calculate a single rate of return based on the most likely pattern of cashflows, but to calculate a range of possible outcomes. Particularly significant vulnerabilities and opportunities can be assessed at the outset, and appropriate contingency and other action plans implemented quickly to ensure the actual return is maximised.

### 6.4.3 Earnings multiple valuation

Current management research shows that earnings multiples valuation techniques are widely used. Despite the popularity, the use of earnings multiples places far too much attention on recent and current profit performance, whereas a sound basis of valuation should concentrate on medium or long-term projections. None the less, valuation using earnings multiples is easy to understand and simple to use. So it represents another method which is suitable for the owners of private businesses and non-accountants to use. The value of a business is calculated on an earnings multiple approach by:

- using the adjusted profit before tax for the previous financial year;
- deducting corporation tax at the full rate, even though the business may have paid tax at the small companies rate, on the assumption that the acquirer will have to pay the full rate of tax in future;

- multiplying the profit after tax for the previous year, calculated as described above, by an appropriate number of years.

One shortcoming of this method is that the valuation is demonstrably dependent on the appropriate number of years chosen for valuation, and this is necessarily somewhat subjective.

The justification for the earnings multiple valuation technique is that it relates the value of unquoted companies, both subsidiaries and private businesses, to similar companies listed on the stock market in the same country. Price/earnings ratios are given in the financial press for stock market listed companies, usually described as a P/E ratio, which is the equivalent of an earnings multiple. The P/E ratios given in the financial press are calculated as follows:

$$\text{P/E ratio} = \frac{\text{present market share price}}{\text{historical earnings per share}}$$

Earnings is the jargon used to describe profits after tax, so the historical earnings per share is calculated by dividing the profits after tax for the previous financial year by the average number of issued shares during that year. For example:

Present market share price = 210p
Profit after tax for previous financial year = £2.1 million
Average number of issued shares = 20 million

$$\text{Earnings per share} = \frac{\text{£2.1 million}}{\text{20.0 million}} = 10.5p$$

$$\text{P/E ratio} = \frac{210p}{10.5p} = 20.0$$

In simple terms, the P/E ratio of 20.0 means that the shares are currently being traded at a price equivalent to 20 times the profit after tax achieved in the previous financial year. Generally speaking, a higher than average P/E ratio means that the shares are more highly valued by investors because they anticipate future growth in earnings per share will be above average.

In general, unquoted companies, both subsidiaries and private companies, are bought and sold at lower earnings multiples than the P/E ratio for a similar listed company with comparable profit growth prospects in the same market sector.

Some owners of private businesses believe that this lower valuation compared with a similar listed company is unfair. It is justified by the fact that there is little or no opportunity to buy and sell shares in an unquoted company. Furthermore, the success of a private business may be unduly dependent on the continued commitment of the present owners. While the acquirer is likely to seek to reduce the risk by negotiating an earn-out deal to maintain the commitment of the owners during the short term, the dependence on owners reduces the worth of a business to prospective purchasers.

Current empirical evidence is that the earnings multiples paid for unquoted companies show a discount of about 30–40 per cent compared to the P/E ratio of quoted companies in the same market sector, with similar prospects for future profit growth. This means that if comparable listed companies have a P/E ratio of 20.0, the earnings multiple applied to an unquoted company would be 30–40 per cent lower, which gives a valuation of 12–14 times the fully taxed profits of the company achieved during the previous year. So that if a business to be acquired made an adjusted and fully taxed profit of £100,000 in the previous financial year, the valuation assuming a comparable listed company P/E ratio of 20 would be between £1.2 million and £1.4 million, reflecting a discount of 30–40 per cent.

Where there is demonstrable scarcity, rarity or uniqueness value, resulting from a lack of suitable businesses to acquire, the discount may be significantly smaller. In exceptional cases businesses have been sold at a premium rather than a discount to the P/E ratios of comparable listed companies. If the company to be acquired is suitable to obtain a stock market listing, the profits are already sufficiently large and there is no reason why it could not obtain a listing quickly, the valuation approach needs to be modified.

Vendors should seek to negotiate a purchase price to reflect the actual P/E ratio which could be achieved on listing, less the total costs involved to acquire a stock market listing. In other words, the aim should be to reject any discount compared with the P/E ratios of similar listed companies or at least to achieve a much smaller discount.

When using earnings multiples techniques for business valuation, vendors should consider whether or not it will be possible to persuade the acquirer to pay a purchase price based on the forecast profits after tax for the current year. Clearly, during the first few months of the financial year a purchaser should reject any valuation based on projected profits for the current year. Historical P/E ratios given in the financial press are based on the audited profit for the previous year and it is too early in the financial year of the target company to justify using current year projections.

On the other hand, if the sale is being negotiated during the final quarter of the financial year, the year will have ended, or nearly so, by the time of legal completion. So there is a stronger justification for the vendors to argue that the valuation should be based on the profit projection for the current year. If the acquirer is persuaded to pay a higher price, there is a case for insisting that the vendors warrant the profit to be achieved and that the contract provides a clawback if the warranted profits are not achieved. As the valuation will represent a multiple of annual profits after tax, it is reasonable that the clawback for any shortfall against warranted profits should be on a similar multiple rather than merely pound for pound reimbursement of the shortfall.

### 6.4.4 Net asset backing

For most profitable manufacturing and service businesses, net asset backing will be a secondary factor to profit and cashflow generation when determining the price to be paid. None the less, asset backing cannot be ignored. In a service business where asset backing is typically low as a percentage of the valuation, such as a public relations consultancy, the initial purchase consideration paid on legal completion is likely to be significantly lower, and the potential to receive earn-out consideration substantially greater, than for a manufacturing company with considerable net tangible assets.

On the other hand, there are businesses making modest profits in relation to the net tangible assets of the business because of a substantial investment in freehold property or expensive capital equipment. As a result, the valuation arrived at using techniques based on profit and cashflow generation described earlier in this chapter may be lower than the net tangible assets of the business. Faced with this situation, vendors should seek to negotiate a purchase price in excess of net tangible asset value in order to receive some premium or goodwill for the profitable business which is being sold. This assumes that it does not make sense for the vendors to extract selected assets before initiating the sale process in order to maximise shareholder value.

When a business is making losses or is in receivership the acquirer should seek to negotiate a price significantly below the current value of net assets at the time of negotiating the purchase. As the company is loss-making, the net tangible asset value of the business will have declined even by legal completion to the extent of losses incurred in the meantime. In most cases, it will be several months at least before losses are eliminated and the break-even point is reached, further diminishing the net asset worth of the business.

Additionally, the acquirer is faced with the costs of installing a suitably experienced chief executive and preferably a finance director as well to achieve the turnround. Furthermore, most experienced company directors will point out that in turnround situations there is a likelihood that unidentified problems will be discovered post-acquisition, which are likely to further decrease the net asset value of the business before the break-even point is reached.

Provided there is no threat of receivership or risk of breaching banking covenants, prospective vendors of loss-making businesses should realise that the chances of selling the business and achieving an acceptable price will be materially increased by eliminating losses first. If there is a possibility of a cashflow crisis, no time should be lost in attempting to sell the business as a going concern, and particularly so if the shareholders of a private business have outstanding personal guarantees in connection with bank borrowings or leasehold obligations.

### 6.4.5 Impact on earnings per share

A key objective for stock market-listed companies is to achieve significant earnings per share growth not only in aggregate over the medium to long term, but annually as well. Experience demonstrates that a profit setback in a year may have a disproportionately large and lingering adverse effect on the share price.

As described earlier, earnings per share are calculated by dividing the profits after tax earned for ordinary shareholders by the number of shares issued.

The undoubted pressure on listed companies to achieve earnings per share growth every year without interruption affects the prices they are prepared to pay for acquisitions. Some listed companies have a deep-rooted psychological resistance to paying a higher multiple for an unquoted company than the present P/E ratio of their own shares. A justifiable concern would be that by paying a higher multiple, this could reduce the earnings per share of the enlarged group depending on the method used to finance the acquisition.

There may be equally logical factors at work as well. The reason why the listed company has a below-average P/E ratio may be because the subsidiaries are in relatively unattractive market sectors or have only limited scope for further profit growth. Faced with this situation, the need may be to acquire businesses in attractive market segments with demonstrable profit growth potential, and because of their attractiveness the prices to be paid will be higher than the current P/E ratio of the bidder.

On the other hand, when a large acquisition is contemplated relative to the size of a listed bidder, there could be unacceptable earnings per share dilution at some stage during the short to medium term. This could happen if an acquisition is to be financed by a rights issue of shares, an institutional placing of shares to realise cash for the vendor, or the issue of convertible loan stock. In these circumstances, the bidder should calculate the projected earnings per share of the enlarged group post-acquisition to ensure there will be no unacceptable dilution throughout the medium term.

## 6.5 Earn-out deals

The valuation of a business and the deal structure proposed for acquisition are interrelated and must be considered together. If the net asset backing of the business is low compared to the overall valuation, the acquirer would be taking an unacceptable risk to pay the full price on legal completion. The fact that the vendors appear enthusiastic to sign, say, a three-year service contract to provide continuity of management should not give rise to comfort. Without the incentive of ownership, it is possible that the former owners will take a relaxed view about the future success of the business. In these circumstances, the acquirer may need to terminate their employment, pay substantial sums for the unexpired part of service contracts and appoint a new management team.

Earn-out deals are a minefield and in a perfect world would not happen because they are disliked by both acquirers and vendors. The reality is quite different. In the majority of private company acquisitions, earn-out deals are a necessary evil. It is often the only way to meet the overall price expectation of the vendors with acceptable protection for the acquirer.

Situations when an earn-out deal may be essential to reach an agreed deal include:

- Low asset backing relative to the business value. In some service companies the net tangible assets may be only about 20 per cent or less of the total business valuation.
- Where the business is particularly dependent upon one customer or client. A successful public relations consultancy business had been formed 14 years ago and the first client represented 35 per cent of total income at the time of sale. The vendors took the view that they had excellent relations with this major client and it would still be a major client in another 14 years' time. Understandably, prospective purchasers rejected this assertion as nothing more than a statement of faith.

  There is a growing tendency for clients to subject existing advisers to a beauty parade against competing firms from time to time. The loss of this client or even a material reduction in the level of business would have turned the company from profit into loss. Quite rightly, the initial purchase consideration payable on legal completion was modest. The earn-out payment was substantial and based on the retention of the major client for a period of three years after legal completion.

- The business may be particularly dependent on only one or two directors. Consider an insurance broking business founded and owned by two directors which has grown substantially to employ nearly 100 staff. In such a situation, it is not unusual for the majority of business to be won by the owner-directors and even the retention of existing clients could be dependent on the personal rapport established by the directors.

In contrast, earn-out deals occur only in a small minority of acquisitions involving a subsidiary or division of a group. It will be assumed that as the directors of the business are salaried employees they would like to continue their employment and there is a much lesser dependence on them compared to owner-directors. The possibility could still exist that the subsidiary or division is particularly dependent on retaining a particular client or customer. Consequently, there have been a few earn-out deals involving subsidiaries or divisions. Almost without exception, the acquirer and vendor have been substantial groups with a mutual respect for each other. Also, the proportion of earn-out consideration compared with initial payment has been small.

A key factor in structuring an earn-out deal is that the initial payment payable on legal completion should be a reasonable rather then a generous sum. If the business is profitable, the acquirer should expect to pay an amount in excess of the current net asset value of the business initially. Otherwise, it is tantamount to seeking to buy the assets at a discount to their current net worth and to acquire a profitable business free of charge. The earn-out payments should be structured so that no additional payment is received unless profits are improved, or at the very least maintained throughout the earn-out period.

Perhaps the prime dislike of both buyers and sellers concerning earn-out deals is the likelihood of disagreement over the profit figure to be used to calculate the earn-out payments. When disagreement occurs over the calculation of profit for earn-out calculation purposes, the intended incentive may become a source of demotivation, leading in extreme cases to time-consuming and costly litigation. The risk and extent of disagreement can be reduced to acceptable levels by ensuring that an exhaustive definition of profit is included in the Sale and Purchase Agreement.

The earn-out should be based on profit before tax, not profit after tax. While group shareholders are rightly concerned to maximise profits after tax, this is best achieved at group level. Furthermore, it avoids the situation whereby a change in the tax regulations reduces the tax liability during the earn-out period and increases the size of the earn-out payment without any achievement or contribution by the vendors. Conversely, if a change in tax regulations increases the tax liability during an earn-out period, many vendors would seek to have the adverse effect of the tax changes set aside for the purposes of calculating earn-out payments. While there is no contractual justification for adopting this approach, a refusal to make any allowance may still result in demotivating the vendors because they feel unfairly treated.

The definition of profit before tax in the Sale and Purchase Agreement should include:

- the accounting policies to be used, because for statutory accounts purposes the group will adopt established group accounting policies immediately following acquisition, which may affect the calculation of profit;
- the acquirer is likely to want to provide certain services to the business during the earn-out period, such as legal advice, payroll and pension administration, insurance, treasury management and the audit to be carried out by group auditors. Either a fixed amount of management charge must be agreed for each year of the earn-out agreement, or an unambiguous basis for calculating the amount to be charged each year must be defined;
- the business may wish to use central services available within the group during the earn-out period, such as warehousing, transportation, desktop publishing, and so on. Charges for these services should reflect usage

and a simple 'rate card' needs to be agreed to arrive at the cost to be charged during the earn-out period;

- the group may have a policy of transfer pricing between different subsidiaries in order to share the profit between them arising from eventual sales to third party customers. One of the reasons for acquiring the business may be that it is a key supplier to some group subsidiaries. The vendors should firmly resist the use of transfer pricing in their business until after the end of the earn-out period, because it could lead to uncertainty and disagreement. The business should be free to sell to other group subsidiaries on a market pricing basis, and to be under no obligation to purchase from other group subsidiaries unless market prices apply;
- some vendors imagine that the group will provide additional finance for capital expenditure and working capital requirements at no cost, which is unrealistic and naive. It is reasonable for the group to charge the current overdraft rate for additional finance provided. Vendors should negotiate that when surplus cash is transferred to the group, an agreed deposit rate of interest will be paid;
- some groups levy a dividend on subsidiaries as a means of centralised cash management. The vendors must reject a situation whereby a dividend levy is applied and the business is charged interest on the additional cash required to grow the business, as a result of paying the dividend.

In an earn-out deal, the vendors have every right to expect that they will provide the managing director throughout the earn-out period. Furthermore, all continuing shareholder directors should seek service contracts for the duration of the earn-out period to ensure that they cannot be dismissed prematurely, which would impair their ability to maximise the deferred consideration. Better still, the service contracts should extend to about four months after the end of the earn-out period so that the shareholder directors know exactly what is happening in the business. This could affect the calculation of the profit in the final year of the earn-out period, such as provisions to be made for doubtful debts, redundant stock, and such like.

It is reasonable for an acquirer to assume that profits should continue to grow during the first two or three years post-acquisition. Consequently, the acquirer should seek to negotiate increased profit thresholds each year before the vendors qualify for any earn-out payment. At the very least, the minimum profit performance to qualify for an earn-out payment should be to maintain the previous year profit or the current year profit forecast as appropriate. None the less, the acquirer may need to agree to some adjustments in the profit thresholds to qualify for earn-out payments where certain requirements are to be imposed upon the way in which the business is managed. These include:

- if the group insists on a qualified finance director being appointed in addition to existing staff, the vendors should seek to have the profit thresholds reduced to reflect the additional cost;
- a key reason for acquiring the business may be to establish an overseas distribution network. It is possible that the vendors may conclude that the likely costs to be incurred are not commensurate with the additional profit which can be achieved during the earn-out period. Consequently, there is a risk that the vendors will seek to minimise and delay relevant expenditure, and a market opportunity may be lost as a consequence. Faced with this possibility, the acquirer should consider reducing the profit thresholds by the actual amount of approved expenditure incurred and ignoring any operating profits or losses achieved during the earn-out period.

It is inadvisable to have an earn-out period of longer than two years from the beginning of the acquirers next financial year. An earn-out period of three years should be regarded as a maximum, unless there is overwhelming evidence on the merits of the particular case to extend the earn-out period for up to five years. The purpose of an earn-out period should be primarily to ensure the commitment of the previous owners to achieve continued profit growth during the critical period after the change of ownership.

By creating an earn-out arrangement, the acquired business must be operated as a self-contained unit in order to calculate the profit on which the earn-out payments are calculated. Consequently, any plans to rationalise or integrate the acquired business with a similar one already owned by the acquiring group may need to be postponed until the end of the earn-out period. If the acquirer helps the acquired business to achieve increased sales by introducing new business, the earn-out will mean that the acquirer will have to pay a multiple of the additional profit by way of increased earn-out payments as a result.

If a relevant acquisition opportunity should arise during the earn-out period, the vendors are unlikely to wish to pursue it because it could distract them from maximising their earn-out payment, even if an adjustment is made to the profit targets to reflect the acquisition.

The business acquired should be required to produce budgets, monthly management accounts and updated year-end forecasts in accordance with group procedures as soon as possible following the acquisition. If this requires additional expenditure, the treatment of the costs involved needs to be agreed for the purpose of calculating earn-out payments. The acquirer should establish board control immediately on legal completion. Monthly board meetings should take place, chaired by the person in the acquiring group accountable for post-acquisition management.

Appropriate group operating procedures should be installed immediately. For example, guidelines for dealing with the media, purchasing authority limits, approval for initiating litigation, and so on. While the vendors should be given ample freedom during the earn-out period, competition with other subsidiaries must be ruled out.

If the business begins to deteriorate, and unless the vendors can demonstrate an ability to retrieve the situation sufficiently quickly, the acquiring company should take control. If the result of this is that the vendors are entitled to receive some earn-out consideration, this is a lesser price to pay than merely to stand by and watch the business fail.

There is no doubt that earn-out arrangements inspire the vendors to adopt a short-term attitude in order to maximise their earn-out consideration. Expenditure may be deferred until after the earn-out period ends, and additional business could be won at reduced profit margins to meet the profit target required. Consequently, it is essential that the maximum earn-out payments are capped to avoid an excessive incentive to the vendors. Ideally, the cap or limit on the earn-out payments should be set so that the maximum consideration can be achieved by the vendors without resorting to measures which will prejudice the success of the business following the end of the earn-out period.

Another measure recommended to protect the acquirer is for deferred payment to be calculated on the aggregate profit for the whole earn-out period. Otherwise there could be a temptation for the vendors to maximise profit in one year, only to fall short of the target in another year and achieve a higher earn-out payment as a result.

### 6.6 Key point summary

1.  There is no such thing as a correct valuation for a business, arguably the only meaningful valuation is the highest amount a purchaser will pay.
2.  The foundation for valuing a business is rigorous projections of profit and cashflows.
3.  The most widely used techniques for valuation are return on investment, discounted cashflow analysis, earnings multiples and net asset backing.
4.  At least two different valuation techniques should be used to avoid any undue bias.
5.  The definition of profit to be used for calculating earn-out payments must be carefully defined in the contract to avoid disagreement later.

# 7 Negotiation

Negotiating the purchase or sale of a business is deceptively complex. Furthermore, negotiation is an art not a science and cannot be reduced to a standardised routine. Knowledge of the relevant taxation and legal regulations in the country concerned is essential, otherwise a seemingly attractive deal may be negotiated with onerous tax consequences or unacceptable legal implications.

Earn-out deals are even more complex. Some people mistakenly think that the formulation of an earn-out deal can be left to experienced lawyers and handled as a routine part of drafting the Sale and Purchase Agreement. This is not the case, because the detailed arrangements of the proposed earn-out deal must be agreed between the buyer and the seller before a lawyer can incorporate them in the legal documentation.

In addition to the legal and tax awareness requirements, the vendors of a private company face the problems of emotional involvement. The stress involved is comparable to that of an acrimonious divorce. Negotiation does not simply involve one meeting, with the rest of the process amounting to nothing more than execution of an agreed deal. In practice, there is more or less continuous negotiation from the first discussion of the proposed deal format through to the day of legal completion.

If either the buyer or the seller does not intend to engage professional advisers to negotiate Heads of Agreement, it is essential that he or she has sufficient legal and tax awareness before the negotiating process begins.

There are two key stages in negotiating the purchase or sale of a business successfully:

- establishing the deal format;
- negotiating the detailed Heads of Agreement.

Each of these will be considered separately.

## 7.1 The deal format

It is quite unsatisfactory – and quite unnecessary – to both buyer and seller for final negotiations to be spread out over a period of several months. Equally, the vendors should avoid being rushed into signing Heads of Agreement at the end of a single negotiation meeting.

The purpose of the first negotiation meeting should be to agree the format of the deal and to set a date for the detailed negotiations to formulate the Heads of Agreement. Although there may have been some general discussion about the basis of a deal at an earlier stage, specific issues may now concern both buyer and seller. The vendors should have appointed corporate finance advisers or, at the very least, have had an initial discussion with their legal advisers. Consequently, various points are likely to have emerged which require some preliminary discussion with the acquirers. The acquirer may wish to structure the deal somewhat differently from that originally envisaged as a result of the initial investigation carried out into the target business.

It is important that significant differences between the two sides should be tabled and discussed before the detailed negotiations take place to formulate the Heads of Agreement. The aim must be to create a basis and mutual expectation to reach agreement during the Heads of Agreement negotiations.

Issues which may need to be raised at the deal format meeting include:

- what is to be bought and sold;
- earn-out deal features;
- retention of assets;
- management issues;
- likely price;
- conditions, warranties and indemnities.

Each of these issues will be considered in turn.

### 7.1.1 What is to be bought and sold

Based on the initial investigation of the business, the purchaser may express a desire to acquire only the assets and business rather than the share capital of the company. In extreme cases, this could be a requirement which is simply non-negotiable. For example, it may have become apparent that there have been a number of significant tax irregularities in the conduct of the business and the purchaser is not prepared to rely on tax indemnities as a satisfactory solution to the problem. Also, there may be a concern that the vendors will transfer the purchase consideration outside their control following the sale, and consequently the indemnity protection could be worthless.

Vendors of private companies must recognise that, from a tax standpoint, the sale of the assets and the business is generally less favourable for them than the sale of the share capital. This is because the sale of the assets and the business invokes the proceeds being taxed twice. The company will have a capital gains tax liability on the sale of the assets; then the individual shareholders will face an additional tax liability on receipt of the cash proceeds from the company.

If the purchaser insists on buying the assets and the business, the vendor should try to negotiate a higher price to compensate for the additional tax liability. It has to be realised, however, that the purchaser may insist that the purchase of the assets and business is essential protection to justify the purchase price offered originally.

A particular subsidiary, division, branch or activity of the business may be of little interest or unattractive to the purchaser. The vendors should pursue the opportunity to exclude it from the sale, because there should be little impact on the purchase price, and either retain the activity or sell it to another purchaser at an attractive price.

In the case of a private company, freehold property may be owned by individual shareholders and used by the business without any formal lease or rental agreement. The vendors may believe that the freehold site has considerable development potential for alternative use at some time in the future and wish to retain the freehold, as purchasers are generally unwilling to take future development potential into account when valuing a business. Outline agreement should be reached on a mutually acceptable period of lease and the annual cost. In these circumstances, the vendors should be prepared to give a lease of at least three years' duration. They must take account of the fact that a one-year lease effectively means that the purchaser must actively relocate the business immediately on legal completion, and this could be unacceptable.

When a subsidiary is sold, the vendor will insist that any reference to group ownership is deleted from the business name, either immediately or within an agreed period. Alternatively, the subsidiary being sold may use patents, trademarks or brand names which will continue to be used elsewhere in the group. In these circumstances, it will be necessary to negotiate the terms of a licence for continued use for defined purposes in certain countries rather than transfer the beneficial ownership.

## 7.1.2 Earn-out deal features

It is possible that although the acquirer originally indicated a willingness to pay the purchase consideration in full on legal completion, insight gained into the business during the initial investigation has caused a change of mind. If it is the case, this should be raised with the vendors at the deal format meeting. The vendors are more likely to accept an earn-out deal when there is time to reflect before the detailed negotiation meeting, but might rule out an earn-out deal completely if the possibility is delayed to the detailed negotiation meeting.

When an earn-out deal has been agreed in principle before the deal format meeting takes place, the vendors should seek some clarification to avoid any unacceptable surprises at the detailed negotiation meeting. It is common-place in earn-out deals that the entire share capital will be purchased at legal completion, but this should be confirmed. If not, the vendors should establish that they will have a contractual put option to oblige the purchaser to buy the remaining equity within a defined period on an agreed valuation formula, in addition to the entitlement to receive deferred purchase consideration as a result of the initial sale of equity.

If the range of the earn-out period has not been agreed before the deal format meeting, it should be discussed at this stage. Generally speaking, a shorter earn-out period is better for the vendors provided that a lower ceiling is not imposed on the maximum deferred consideration payable. Vendors should resist earn-out periods longer than two years after the end of the acquirer's current financial year. Vendors tend to find that they work harder than ever during an earn-out period in order to maximise the deferred purchase consideration.

Most importantly, the approximate amount of purchase consideration payable on legal completion needs to be discussed. Earn-out deals have been completed where the proportion of deferred purchase consideration has ranged from below 10 per cent to over 90 per cent of the maximum deal value. Given this wide range, vendors must ensure that the proportion of consideration to be payable at legal completion is acceptable, before the final negotiations take place.

### 7.1.3 Retention of assets

Some private companies own assets which are not essential to the running of the business. Boats, aeroplanes, race horses and expensive motor cars come into this category. At the deal format stage, the question of these assets needs to be discussed. The vendors may wish to buy the assets; alternatively, the purchaser may require the vendors to buy them because a sale may prove difficult. Vendors should recognise that assets of this kind need to be purchased at sensible prices. It is unacceptable to reduce the purchase price of the business so that the personal assets may be purchased for a nominal sum. This would reduce the capital gains tax liability on the vendors, but scrutiny by the Inland Revenue would lead to an additional tax liability at some stage following legal completion. Acquirers must firmly reject this, and vendors should not even request it, because the practice amounts to tax evasion.

### 7.1.4 Management issues

Management continuity is an important issue for acquirers, unless the business is making a loss and a new managing director is to be appointed to revitalise the business and reduce staff levels. When the purchase consideration is to be paid in full on legal completion, the acquirer should obtain an oral commitment from each director in a private company of a minimum period of continued employment. Acquirers should draw no comfort from

- the team leader will introduce each individual and outline the different roles;
- the emphasis will be on listening;
- responses and intervention will be measured, the team leader will invite individuals to contribute to ensure a controlled approach;
- no one will interrupt when a member of the other side is speaking, because valuable information and insight may be lost;
- when a question is asked of the other side, the person will be encouraged to answer it in full, and supplementary questions may be raised when appropriate;
- the team leader will interrupt or curtail other team members whenever appropriate;
- a friendly and firm approach will be adopted;
- sarcasm, point scoring, bad temper and irritation should be avoided.

Before the negotiation meeting, each side should prepare a draft agenda. Once the preliminary remarks have been made by each side, the next step should be to agree a detailed agenda designed to ensure that all the issues needed to produce a meaningful agreement will be discussed and resolved. When dealing with the shareholders of a private company, the acquirer should encourage them to raise any issue which they regard as significant for whatever reason, because once Heads of Agreement have been negotiated it is acceptable to introduce additional items for negotiation.

A typical agenda for negotiating comprehensive Heads of Agreement can include:

- update of events since the last meeting;
- confirmation of what is to be purchased;
- purchase of personal assets by directors;
- property leases;
- transfer of pension fund;
- intellectual property rights;
- removal of personal guarantees;
- conditions, warranties and indemnities;
- service contracts and consultancy agreements;
- earn-out period, threshold and formula;
- purchase price and consideration;
- timetable to legal completion.

Each of these items will be considered in turn.

## 7.2.1 Update of events since the last meeting

Heads of Agreement negotiation meetings are quite often unduly tense affairs. This is counter-productive. The opportunity to update the other side on events since the last meeting is an important preliminary, and serves as an effective ice-breaker as well. The vendor should take the opportunity to demonstrate continued progress in the business since the last meeting. Relevant information, which can be presented briefly, can include:

- management accounts for the previous month;
- sales figures and orders received to date for the current month;
- an updated sales and profit forecast for the current financial year;
- significant new customers or orders received;
- recent events such as a branch opening or a new product launch;
- any important media coverage received.

The acquirer should be concerned if the most recent set of monthly management accounts is overdue. This may be an attempt to hide a disappointing performance in the previous month. If this happens, friendly but firm questioning should establish the cause of the delay and obtain reassurance that performance has not deteriorated.

### 7.2.2 Confirmation of what is to be purchased

While what is to be purchased should have been agreed at the deal format meeting, it is desirable to rehearse this again briefly to avoid any confusion. This may seem pedantic, but the reality is that a number of Heads of Agreement have been rendered worthless because of inaccurate assumptions or confusion over what was to be purchased.

### 7.2.3 Purchase of personal assets by directors

Assets primarily for the personal use of the directors, such as a boat, to be purchased by them should have been agreed at the deal format meeting. In the meantime, the acquirer should have made enquiries to establish the likelihood of being able to sell these assets to a third party if necessary, the time required and the probable price to be obtained. In reaching agreement with the directors on the price to be paid, the acquirer should take the opportunity to outline the likely price to be obtained from an external purchaser. In this way, the financial benefit to the vendor from purchasing the assets should be pointed out, or better still agreed on, so that this amount is taken into account in the overall value of the deal.

### 7.2.4 Property leases

If a freehold property owned by the company is to be excluded from the sale, because the vendor wishes to benefit from possible redevelopment in the future, the purchase price or a suitable lease need to be agreed. Discussion on the terms of the lease should be restricted to the type, the duration, the annual value and rent review dates. The objective is simply to provide the lawyer with the key details necessary to draft a lease agreement.

Another situation requiring a lease agreement to be prepared is when the ownership of a freehold property used by the business is to be retained by the vendor.

### 7.2.5 Transfer of pension fund

The transfer from a group pension fund when a subsidiary or division is being sold is a problematic issue. It may take a lengthy period to agree the value of the fund to be transferred to meet the pension entitlement of both current and previous employees. Acquirers are likely to find it difficult to persuade the vendor to share any surplus fund value to benefit the employees being transferred. In some cases, where it has not been possible to reach agreement on the fund value to be transferred, it has been decided to leave the vendor group to meet the outstanding entitlement of both current and previous employees, and for the acquirer to invite staff currently employed either to join an existing scheme or to create a new one for them as appropriate.

Although the resolution of pension issues is long-winded, both the acquirer and the vendor should avoid incurring any costs for professional advice until the Heads of Agreement have been negotiated. Otherwise, the expense may prove to be abortive. At the time of legal completion it is possible that pension matters have not been resolved, but a process and timetable for resolving them have been established.

### 7.2.6 Intellectual property rights

When a group sells a subsidiary or division, it may be necessary to license the use of intellectual property such as patents, trademarks and brand names because these are used elsewhere in the vendor group. The licence period and any cost of renewal should be agreed during the heads of negotiation meeting, and the detailed arrangements left to the lawyers.

### 7.2.7 Removal of personal guarantees

The shareholders of a private company may have given personal guarantees either to secure bank finance or in connection with a property lease. Quite rightly, they will want these guarantees removed as soon as possible after legal completion, but it should be recognised that the acquirer can only give an undertaking to use best endeavours because it rests with the bank or landlord to accept alternative arrangements. Vendors should take comfort from the fact that the term 'best endeavours' places a strong onus on the acquirer to do whatever can be done to remove the personal guarantees.

### 7.2.8 Conditions, warranties and indemnities

A warranty is an undertaking by a vendor to a purchaser that a specific state of affairs exists in the business for sale. If the warranty is inaccurate and the purchaser suffers actual loss as a result, he or she is entitled to sue the vendor for damages for breach of contract.

Warranties fulfil two principal functions: first, they form part of the overall due diligence exercise by flushing out specific areas of concern when the first draft of the Sale and Purchase Agreement is circulated; second, they are the mechanism by which an acquirer modifies the legal principle of caveat emptor – i.e. the burden falls on a purchaser to satisfy itself that a target business is as the vendor says. Through comprehensive warranty cover, a purchase can shift that burden significantly by requiring the vendor to disclose any areas of potential risk within the business.

Indemnities have a different function. Certain issues – in particular tax – are of sufficient concern that a purchaser needs more reassurance than a warranty can provide. An indemnity ensures that if following the purchase a significant liability arises, the purchaser does not need to prove that he or she has suffered loss in a court of law (as with a warranty claim) but can simply require the vendor to repay him or her in full for whatever cost the purchaser has had to bear.

Warranties and indemnities take up many pages in a typical Sale and Purchase Agreement, and some of them are long-established safeguards for acquirers, which are generally acceptable to vendors. Consequently, it would be premature and far too time-consuming even to agree a list of the detailed warranties and indemnities during a Heads of Agreement negotiation meeting. None the less, the vendors should ensure that the acquirer identifies any unusual or onerous warranties and indemnities. In this way, the acquirer is largely denied the opportunity to introduce warranties and indemnities in the contract which come as an unpleasant or unacceptable surprise to the vendors.

A key issue surrounding warranties and indemnities is the maximum exposure of the shareholders. Conventional wisdom among many solicitors is that the maximum exposure (*de maximis*) should be the total value of the consideration paid. However, vendors should work hard to establish that the maximum liability resulting from warranties and indemnities should be the estimated purchase proceeds net of capital gains tax. Vendors should regard it as unthinkable to accept a higher liability, because this would mean that they could be worse off financially as a result of selling the company.

It should be recognised that the maximum exposure must always be negotiated on the merits of the particular case. Vendors should negotiate hard to achieve a lower level of exposure. A way of tackling this issue is to persuade the acquirer to identify the risks faced and to quantify the likely loss from each one. In many cases, this will produce an aggregate figure substantially lower than the net of tax purchase proceeds received by the vendors.

Another issue which should be negotiated during the Heads of Agreement meeting is the *de minimis* limits for claims under warranties and indemnities. It is in the interests of both the acquirer and the vendor to agree on a large enough minimum figure before the vendors are liable to make a payment under the warranty and indemnity protection. Otherwise it is possible that both sides could be involved in costly litigation, which is not justified by the size of the claim.

The duration of tax indemnities sometimes becomes an emotionally charged issue. The standard period for tax indemnities selected by most lawyers is six years to reflect current Inland Revenue practice. Vendors are often anxious that they face a potential liability for such a long period after they have sold their business, even though the liability is restricted to events which happened prior to legal completion. If it becomes a deal-breaking issue, there is a possible case for the acquirer to accept a reduced period of only two years for tax indemnities. However, many companies and professional advisers would reject this. During this time the acquirer will have completed two annual audits of the business, and if there is a tax liability relating to the period prior to legal completion it should be discovered during this period, particularly as the audit of a newly acquired company should pay particular attention to discovering any breaches of warranties and indemnities.

### 7.2.9 Service contracts and consultancy agreements

The acquirer of a private company will be keen to ensure that salaries, company cars, pension contributions and other fringe benefits of continuing directors and staff are in line with group policy. Shareholder directors of private companies should recognise the importance of this to an acquiring group, and be content that the profit will have been increased correspondingly for valuing the business.

When an earn-out deal is involved, the continuing directors of a private company should insist on a service contract which ensures their employment not only to the end of the agreed earn-out period but sufficiently beyond that date to enable the annual accounts to be prepared while they are still employed in the business.

In some private companies, a senior executive may have negotiated an eccentric profit share agreement, which the acquirer finds unacceptable. In these circumstances, the acquirer should insist on renegotiating the agreement in line with established group policy shortly before legal completion. If it is necessary to buy out the existing agreement by a lump-sum payment, there is a strong case for deducting this from the agreed purchase consideration.

The purchaser may wish a director to leave immediately on legal completion, contrary to his wishes. If the director is not a shareholder, the vendors should insist that the acquirer pays a suitable retirement package in addition to the agreed purchase consideration. In the case of a private company, when the person asked to retire is a shareholder, the acquirer has a case for rejecting any additional payment on the basis that the increased profit has been reflected in the overall valuation of the business.

Conversely, a director in a private company may wish to retire from full-time employment on legal completion, but be keen to have a consultancy agreement as part of the overall purchase consideration in order to provide a continuing income. If this is agreed by the acquirer, the duties to be carried out, the time to be spent, the duration of the agreement and the payment of expenses should be agreed during the heads of negotiation meeting. It is important that the remuneration is commensurate with the work to be undertaken, otherwise the Inland Revenue could challenge the agreement. Vendors need to recognise this and be ready to accept a reasonable reward for a consultancy agreement.

### 7.2.10 Earn-out period, threshold and formula

It is worth repeating that earn-out deals are a potential minefield for both vendors and acquirers. This does not stop some people from drifting into an ill-considered earn-out deal. A dangerous situation occurs when the two parties realise only at the heads of negotiation meeting that there is a significant gap between their respective price expectations. While any significant difference on price should have been identified at the deal format meeting, failure to do this is a trap which people fall into. Consequently, the purchaser may suggest a brief adjournment while an earn-out deal is formulated to overcome the problem. This is likely to result in an ill thought out earn-out arrangement, amended, but not necessarily improved on, in negotiation with the vendors.

If an earn-out deal is to be adopted, the purchaser should formulate the arrangements before the heads of negotiation meeting and evaluate the implications by using financial modelling to test possible outcomes.

The first step in formulating an earn-out deal is to decide, or better still to agree, the length of the earn-out period before any formula is devised. There is a danger to the acquirer, that if the vendor succeeds in altering the earn-out period – making it either longer or shorter – the maximum earn-out payment may be significantly easier to achieve.

Whenever an earn-out period is amended, the earn-out formula should be completely reformulated, and not merely extended or shortened. The next step should be to define profit and any charges to be made by the acquirer against profit in precise detail, as set out in Chapter 6. Precision and clarity of thought at this stage should prevent time-consuming argument or costly litigation later.

Only when the earn-out period and the definition of profit for earn-out payments have been agreed should profit targets be outlined. Vendors must recognise that if a reasonable price is to be paid for the business at legal completion, reflecting the performance to date and net asset backing, any earn-out payments should depend on improved profit performance. Vendors should seek to negotiate a constant profit threshold throughout the earn-out period, based on maintaining the profit forecast for the current financial year. Purchasers should press for rising profit thresholds each year because it is reasonable to expect some sustained profit growth throughout the earn-out period, which does not merit any additional purchase consideration.

The next stage is to define the formula for calculating earn-out payments and the ceiling to be placed on the maximum earn-out consideration to be paid.

Inexperienced acquirers and vendors alike find it surprising that standard earn-out formulas or models do not exist. The reason is that each acquisition is so different that every case must be considered individually. In some cases, a lump sum may be payable for achieving a profit threshold set for each year, together with a multiple for every pound of profit achieved in excess of the threshold. It is desirable to base the earn-out consideration on the aggregate profit achieved during the whole earn-out period. This avoids the vendors manipulating the profit in one year to receive the maximum payment in that year, knowing that no earn-out payment is likely to be achieved in another year.

## 7.3 Purchase price and consideration

It is important to the acquirer that all the features of the deal described earlier in this chapter should be resolved before negotiating the amount of purchase consideration payable on legal completion. Otherwise, if the initial purchase price is agreed at the outset of the meeting, and then it becomes obvious that the vendors are negotiating hard or insisting on some peripheral benefits as part of the deal, the overall cost of the acquisition could increase. Provided there has been some meaningful discussion on the purchase price at the deal format stage, it should be possible to persuade the vendors that it is reasonable to delay finalising the price until the other issues have been resolved. Also, the vendors should protect themselves by pointing out that while agreement is being reached on each individual issue, they reserve the right to renegotiate any items when the entire agenda has been addressed.

The form of purchase consideration preferred by the vendor, particularly to minimise or defer capital gains tax liabilities wherever possible, needs to be agreed as part of the Heads of Agreement meeting. Vendors must realise that, in general, tax-advantageous deal structuring for one party is likely to have a tax disadvantage to the other. It is hard to think of examples where a deal can be structured in a way that both buyer and seller automatically profit from the arrangements. Vendors must not assume that once the Heads of Agreement have been negotiated and signed, the acquirer will agree to changes in the deal structure or in the form of purchase consideration in order to minimise tax for the vendors. The acquirer may either reject the proposals or seek to negotiate a quid pro quo in exchange to offset the tax disadvantage incurred by agreeing to the vendor's request.

It is worth repeating that the negotiators for both buyer and seller at the Heads of Agreement meeting must be sufficiently knowledgeable to construct a deal which is both tax-efficient and legally sound. Having made this point, it is inappropriate to attempt to define the detailed mechanisms to be used to achieve a tax-efficient deal during the Heads of Agreement meeting. The mechanics should be sorted out at a later stage by expert tax advisers. The key factor is that a tax-efficient deal structure should have been agreed on before Heads of Agreement are signed.

Vendors are rightly concerned to structure a deal which minimises and defers capital gains tax liabilities as much as possible. Consequently, the choice of purchase consideration is often determined by the opportunities for tax-effectiveness, and this is dealt with in Chapter 8.

## 7.4 Timetable to legal completion

It is important for vendors that the Heads of Agreement meeting defines a detailed timetable to legal completion. An oral assurance to complete the deal within, say, the next six weeks is insufficient. Vendors need to have interim stages and deadlines agreed so that any slippage can be quickly recognised and raised with the acquirer.

The financing arrangements which the acquirer plans to use should be known to the vendors because these can have a significant delay on legal completion. For example, if the acquirer is to raise the finance by a rights issue, it is possible that it is planned to complete two or three acquisitions simultaneously in order to justify raising sufficient cash to make a rights issue worthwhile.

Consequently, there is a risk that if the other acquisitions are either delayed or fail to proceed to legal completion, the vendor's deal could be delayed or put in jeopardy. Another possibility is that the vendors are to be paid on legal completion in cash from the proceeds of a placing of shares on behalf of the vendors to institutional investors. The vendors should ask to what extent the stockbroker to the acquirer has been informed about the proposed acquisition, and request evidence supporting the claim that the shares can be placed without difficulty. The situation must be avoided whereby, shortly before legal completion, the acquirer announces that the stockbroker regards the acquisition as too expensive and a lower purchase price must be accepted in order for the shares to be placed. This is less likely to happen in the case of a sizeable listed group, but it does happen occasionally with smaller listed companies.

Vendors must establish whether or not the acquirer will need to issue a circular to shareholders because the transaction requires shareholder consent or notification. If a circular is required, legal completion may be delayed by some weeks.

When there is no need for a rights issue, a share placing on behalf of the vendors or a Stock Exchange circular, legal completion should take place five or six weeks after signing Heads of Agreement. The acquirer will wish to assume management control of the company as soon as possible after the due diligence and legal work can be completed, without taking any shortcuts.

The Inland Revenue has a period of up to 30 days in which to give tax clearances or to request further information. While it might be tempting to vendors to achieve legal completion in the shortest possible time, it is important to allow sufficient time to obtain tax clearances and for the clearance application to be fully comprehensive so that further information is not requested, which would result in another 30 days' time limit commencing. In this way, the vendors should have much greater peace of mind that the Inland Revenue will not challenge the deal after legal completion, with the result that the vendors could face a significantly higher tax liability than anticipated.

When the acquirer is a private company, the method of financing is just as important. For example, the finance may be provided by a venture capitalist taking an equity stake in the enlarged business and providing some debt finance as well. Alternatively, the acquirer may be planning to obtain a bank loan.

In both cases, the provider of finance will wish to appoint investigating accountants to carry out due diligence. Legal completion may take longer than 5–6 weeks. It is essential that the vendor should find out what progress has been made to reach agreement in principle with the provider of the finance required.

If the acquirer intends to shop around for finance once Heads of Agreement have been signed, there must be some doubt about the likelihood of achieving legal completion. Vendors need to enquire about the method of financing and the progress achieved to date before the Heads of Agreement meeting takes place. It should be quite unacceptable to any vendor to negotiate Heads of Agreement merely on the tacit expectation that the acquirer will be able to raise the finance.

The outline timetable to legal completion should specify the date by which:

- Heads of Agreement will be signed;
- the draft legal agreement will be received from the acquirer;
- due diligence will commence;
- the on-site due diligence work will have been completed;

- due diligence reports will be received by the acquirer;
- formal board approval will have been given for the acquisition;
- the disclosure statement will be received by the acquirer;
- principals and advisers will meet to finalise the legal documentation;
- legal completion will take place.

The timetable to legal completion is so important that each step will be considered in turn.

There is a strong case for not signing Heads of Agreement at the end of the negotiation meeting. This may seem surprising given that the meeting should have articulated in meaningful detail the features of the deal to be encompassed in the Heads of Agreement. The reality is that people may be tired at the end of the meeting, and it makes sense to allow them to reflect on what has been agreed. However, this must not be regarded by either side as an opportunity for a change of mind on certain issues or to introduce additional points.

There is no need for the Heads of Agreement to be drafted by a lawyer. They should be written in commercial language, vetted by a lawyer, and serve as the basis of instruction to the lawyers for both parties when preparing and negotiating the Sale and Purchase Agreement. When lawyers are used to draft the Heads of Agreement, the two sets of lawyers often disagree. This is a pointless exercise which causes unnecessary delay and avoidable expense. It is much better that the lawyers are involved directly only with the Sale and Purchase Agreement.

This does emphasise, however, the need for both the buyer and seller to have sufficient legal and tax knowledge during the negotiations. But it does not necessarily mean that lawyers or tax experts need to be involved. The inclusion of lawyers and tax experts in the negotiation meeting often provokes time-consuming debate on technical issues prematurely and even introduces unnecessary disagreement at this stage. The objective ought to be to reach a comprehensive agreement in commercial terms in an atmosphere of goodwill.

Typically, the Heads of Agreement should be signed within one or two working days of the negotiation meeting. If the vendors wish to take longer than a week to sign the Heads of Agreement, the acquirer must press to identify the cause of the delay. General approval from the shareholders or the group board should have been given to the team negotiating the Heads of Agreement; therefore, it should only be a question of rubber-stamping the final outcome. It is important to the acquirer that the vendors should sign a binding agreement as quickly as possible, prohibiting them from any discussions with other prospective purchasers or announcing the proposed acquisition without the specific approval of the acquirer.

The Sale and Purchase Agreement, which is normally prepared by the acquirer, should be issued as quickly as possible after the Heads of

Agreement have been signed. A period of two working days may seem to be a counsel of perfection, but it should not take longer than five working days. The vendors should insist on receiving the Sale and Purchase Agreement at least two working days before on-site due diligence work is to be commenced, so that their lawyers can be satisfied that onerous conditions have not been included in the contract, which were not raised during the Heads of Agreement meeting. Should this happen, the vendors should immediately take up these matters and resolve them before allowing due diligence to commence.

Vendors need to recognise that staff are likely to realise that the business is being sold at an early stage during the due diligence process. This tends to happen even when the due diligence team present themselves under a different guise, at the request of the vendors.

The arrangements for the due diligence work should be a matter of concern to the vendors. In addition to knowing when the work is to commence, it is important to know how many people will be visiting the company premises and for how long. If the due diligence work appears excessive, the vendors should ask for the acquirer's terms of reference. The vendors should be satisfied that detailed due diligence work is not being carried out on aspects of the business which are not reflected in the Heads of Agreement. Otherwise, there is a risk that the acquirer is simply looking for a justification to renegotiate the deal already agreed.

The vendors should ensure that the due diligence team will announce their arrival at company premises with discretion. A surveyor announcing at reception that he or she has come to carry out a property valuation is exactly the sort of behaviour that creates speculation among staff. Discussion should take place about the extent to which any work could be carried out by the investigating accountants at the offices of the auditors, and whether or not it makes sense to hire a room in a nearby hotel to minimise the time spent on company premises.

It is reasonable for the vendors to ask the acquirer to set a deadline for the receipt of due diligence reports. This enables the vendor to telephone the acquirer a couple of days later to confirm that nothing of significance was revealed during due diligence. If the acquirer is intending to use the due diligence reports as a basis for renegotiation, it is important that the vendor is aware of this as soon as possible.

No time must be lost in addressing the points raised, otherwise delay in legal completion is almost certain because the acquirer is likely to halt the legal work on the transaction until the deal has been renegotiated. Faced with this situation, the vendor should seek to reassure the acquirer about the points raised in the due diligence report. Investigating accountants are negative by nature, driven by their concern to avoid a claim for professional negligence against them. It is quite possible that the investigating accountants have either misunderstood some aspect of the business or have placed undue significance on it, which has concerned the acquirer unnecessarily. Better still, the vendors should have made clear at the Heads of Agreement meeting that if the acquirer seeks to renegotiate the deal in the light of due diligence, they will withdraw from the deal and leave the acquirer to pay for his or her abortive professional costs.

It may seem irrelevant to set a date for formal approval of the acquisition by the board of the acquirer, particularly if the managing director or a main board director has been involved in negotiating the Heads of Agreement. However, some acquirers have used the dubious tactic that the value of the deal must be reduced by a given amount in view of the outcome of the board meeting, if the vendors wish to sell the business. Reasons put forward have included a statement that the managing director was surprised to find that the non-executive directors regarded the purchase price as excessive, or that a main board director was instructed by the board to reduce the offer.

The disclosure letter is a particularly important part of any sale, and its significance is often underestimated by buyers and sellers alike. A prime purpose for the inclusion of comprehensive warranties in the Sale and Purchase Agreement is to ensure that the vendors disclose any situations or aspects of the business which would breach the warranties.

Put simply, it is an effective means of flushing out information which the vendors may have withheld, have been deliberately vague about or did not think it important to mention. Some vendors are reluctant to disclose breaches of warranties because this could jeopardise the deal or lead to renegotiation. This is nonsense. It is a recipe for costly litigation after legal completion, when the acquirer discovers the true facts.

The acquirer needs to review the disclosure letter with the utmost care, because it forms part of the Sale and Purchase Agreement. The acquirer's protection built into the Sale and Purchase Agreement through the warranties is diluted by any disclosures which are made, and these become part of the legal documentation. If the acquirer allows the vendors to make sweeping disclosure statements, the protection of the legal agreement may be substantially diluted. The acquirer should respond to a disclosure letter by seeking to make the disclosures more specific, to renegotiate the deal or to withdraw completely if a material item had been concealed.

An adequate response to the disclosure letter by the acquirer needs time. It is highly desirable that the complete disclosure letter is received by the acquirer at least five working days before legal completion. It is unsatisfactory to allow a situation whereby the vendor presents the disclosure letter at the meeting to sign the documentation for legal completion. Part of the problem is that inexperienced acquirers tend to think that a disclosure letter will be relatively brief. Quite often the disclosure letter amounts to a briefcase full of documents, reports and miscellaneous correspondence.

Lawyers seem to delight in reaching disagreement over a number of points in the Sale and Purchase Agreement. An effective and speedy way to resolve these points is to have a date prearranged for the principals and their advisers to negotiate every outstanding point and agree the wording to be used in a single meeting. While principals often try to avoid legal negotiation meetings, there really is no alternative. Principals can generally make an on the spot commercial decision on a point which lawyers can fail to reach agreement on. If this takes 12 hours – and sometimes it does – so be it. A failure to agree a date for such a meeting during the Heads of Agreement negotiations will inevitably lead to delay. By the time the lawyers have reached disagreement over the documentation, the inability of people to meet at short notice will delay legal completion.

When the acquirer is a large listed group or an overseas corporation, the date of legal completion, and occasionally even the location and time of day, becomes important. A duly authorised board member, and not any board member, must be available to sign the legal documentation because this would normally be the person accountable for the acquisition. When people are involved in overseas travel, booking a space in their diaries to ensure availability for legal completion is important.

## 7.5  Key point summary

1.  There are two key stages in negotiating the purchase or sale of a business successfully, establishing the format of the deal and a separate meeting to formulate the detailed Heads of Agreement.
2.  The deal format discussion should create a basis and mutual expectation to reach agreement during the Heads of Agreement negotiations.
3.  Each side should have a pre-negotiation meeting to agree individual roles and ground rules for conducting the Heads of Agreement meeting.
4.  A detailed agenda should be agreed at the beginning of the Heads of Agreement meeting to ensure every significant item will be addressed.
5.  A comprehensive disclosure statement should be made by vendors and rigorously scrutinised by the acquirer, with amendments negotiated where appropriate.

# 8 Tax issues

When individual shareholders are negotiating the sale of a private company, their principal preoccupation is often to minimise or defer capital gains tax. But by the time of the sale, it may be too late to obtain some of the tax savings which could have been obtained by planning ahead and taking action earlier. As a general rule, action should be taken before a written offer is received for the business, otherwise the tax authorities may challenge the arrangements as a tax-evasion device. Not only is timely action important, but good intentions are not enough.

The action taken must be meticulously executed in accordance with the detailed tax regulations. Even where the principle or intention is valid, the tax authorities will be ready to attack arrangements which have not been carried out in accordance with the regulations. Expert tax advice should be taken and expert help obtained to make the arrangements. Otherwise it may be several months after legal completion before the vendors realise that the tax-saving arrangements they have made are under attack.

When buying or selling a business overseas, it is essential that tax advice is taken locally. A detailed knowledge of the tax rules is not enough. It is essential to know the current way in which the tax authorities are interpreting and implementing the regulations. A tax expert in one country should not be expected to provide reliable advice on an overseas transaction, simply by studying the local tax rules. Furthermore, it must be recognised that in most countries the tax regulations are subject to widespread changes annually, and sometimes more often.

## 8.1 Capital gains tax liability

A capital gains tax liability is assessed on the difference between the sale proceeds and the acquisition cost or valuation of the shares. In the UK, under the legislation in force when writing this book, for shares held at 31 March 1982 the capital gain is calculated by reference to the agreed market valuation of the shares at that date. Individual shareholders in private companies may find that the Inland Revenue will seek to apply a substantial discount when valuing shareholdings under 25 per cent, and this will increase the chargeable gain.

Indexation relief is available to shareholders. This reduces the chargeable gain, but cannot be used to create a loss to offset against other capital gains. Indexation relief is calculated on either the agreed value of the shares at March 1982 or the acquisition cost for shares acquired later. The indexation factor since March 1982 is approaching 100 per cent.

## 8.2 Transfer of shares

A gift of shares to the shareholder's spouse does not crystallise either gain or loss for tax purposes. Consequently, shares could be transferred to a spouse before offers for the business are received in order to take advantage of any unused capital gains tax annual exemption and to ensure full use is made of the lower rate tax bands.

Similarly, there may be some scope to make tax-efficient gifts to other relatives to utilise their annual exemptions and lower rate tax bands.

A more valuable capital gains tax saving can be achieved when both spouses hold shares dating from before April 1982. By transferring a minority shareholding to a spouse, it may mean that all the shares will be treated as a majority holding, deemed to be effective from before April 1982, thus substantially increasing the valuation of shares for capital gains tax purposes. For example, consider individual holdings of 40 per cent and 20 per cent of the shares by the spouses. Gifting the shares to create a single holding of 60 per cent will mean that all the shares are valued more highly as a majority shareholding for capital gains tax purposes, and so the tax liability will be reduced.

In theory, it is possible to take advantage of the fact that there is no capital gains tax liability on death and there is full inheritance tax relief on qualifying shareholdings in trading companies. This would involve transferring shares to elderly or terminally ill relatives, so that these shares could be willed back on death at market value and eliminate the capital gains tax liability at that date. Most people are likely to find this approach too callous and calculating to pursue, and it needs to be remembered that wills can be changed.

## 8.3 Becoming non-resident or domiciled abroad

An individual not resident or not ordinarily resident in the UK escapes UK capital gains tax, except on assets used within a UK trade. This only produces a tax saving, however, when the tax regime in which the shareholder is resident is more favourable than that in the UK.

Non-resident status is not a matter of personal opinion or belief. The Inland Revenue enforces detailed regulations concerning non-residence and the rules must be complied with in every detail and in a timely way. Non-residence can be achieved by working abroad full time under a contract of employment which extends beyond a complete tax year and during which no duties (except incidental duties) are performed in the UK. For most shareholders in a private company, however, the acquirer will require them to continue in full-time employment for a period after legal completion. Also, most shareholders would not find it easy to obtain qualifying employment abroad.

For shareholders choosing to live abroad without qualifying employment, it will be necessary to demonstrate that they have left the UK permanently, have rented or purchased accommodation abroad and remain absent from the UK for at least three years. A provisional ruling on non-residence will only be confirmed by the Inland Revenue after an absence of three years. In the meantime there are strict limits on the time spent visiting the UK.

A shareholder who is resident in the UK but is regarded as domiciled abroad for tax purposes will not be liable to UK capital gains tax arising from overseas gains, provided these are not remitted to the UK.

## 8.4 Retirement relief

Valuable retirement relief is available for shareholders aged 55 or over on the sale of their business, or earlier if retirement is caused by ill health. The current relief is that the first £250,000 of capital gain is tax-free, and the liability is reduced by half on the next £750,000 of gain. At present tax rates (1995/6), this represents a net tax saving of £250,000 on a £1 million gain, and is available on the gift of a business asset as well as on a sale.

The business must be a trading company, and a minimum holding of 5 per cent of the shares is required for retirement relief. The shareholder must have worked as a full-time director or employee for at least one year. If a husband and wife own qualifying shareholdings in a family business, but only one of them is employed full time, only one person will qualify for retirement relief. Faced with this situation, thought should be given to gifting shares as far in advance of the sale as possible with the aim of taking full advantage of the relief on the first £1 million of chargeable gain. The relief is reduced pro rata when someone has not been a shareholder and a director or employee for ten years prior to the sale of the business.

Retirement relief does not apply to chargeable non-business assets, such as an investment property which is not used for the conduct of the business, and it may make sense to sell these assets prior to the sale of the business. Quite often a freehold property used rent free by a private business in its trade is owned by the shareholders as individuals outside the company. Provided the property and the share capital are sold at the same time, both will qualify for retirement relief.

Shareholders should think carefully before deciding to sell their shareholding shortly before their fifty-fifth birthday. If an unsolicited approach to buy the business results in a particularly attractive offer, and the acquirer is not prepared to wait for a shareholder to reach 55, an assessment must be made as to whether or not the offer is sufficiently attractive to offset the loss of retirement relief.

## 8.5 Capital gains tax deferment by reinvestment relief

Reinvestment relief applies to disposals in a qualifying trading company made after 15 March 1993. The gain may be reinvested in the shares of other qualifying unquoted trading companies, and the gain is rolled over or deferred until the shares are sold. If the shares are held until age 55, retirement relief can be claimed if the relevant conditions are met. Alternatively, the capital gains tax liability will disappear if the shares are owned at death. Only the gain needs to be reinvested to obtain relief, not the full proceeds from the disposal of shares. Reinvestment must take place up to one year before disposal and within three years after the disposal, and UK residency is required.

Detailed rules set out exactly what kind of unquoted trading company qualifies for reinvestment relief, and there are specific requirements concerning the future conduct of the qualifying business.

## 8.6 Paper for paper relief

When the shareholder receives shares in the acquiring company there is no chargeable gain until the newly acquired shares are sold. For capital gains tax purposes the new shares are deemed to have the same cost as the old shares. The rules require that the acquiring company should hold 25 per cent of the share capital of the company being acquired, or will have control resulting from a general offer for the shares. The purchase consideration may be a combination of ordinary shares, loan stock and cash. The cost of the original holding would be allocated on a pro rata basis to the cash, newly acquired ordinary shares and loan stock, but the cash element would crystallise a capital gains tax liability. Loan stock must not be redeemable for at least six months to qualify for paper for paper relief.

Once again, expert advice is required to execute the mechanics involved tax-effectively. For example, if the purchase consideration is deemed to be a qualifying corporate bond, then significant differences of tax treatment may result.

## 8.7 Tax-effective purchase consideration

A large pension payment to a company pension scheme or a personal pension scheme prior to the sale of a business will be tax-free, provided the appropriate conditions are met. Vendors should consider making any intended pension payments before initiating the sale process, because as the acquirer is likely to value a profitable business on the basis of profit rather than net asset backing it could be that the reduction in the offer for the business would be less than the amount of the pension payment. If the vendors request the agreement of the purchaser to make pension payments during the negotiation process, undoubtedly the acquirer will expect his or her offer to be reduced equal to the amount of the proposed pension payments.

The payment of a pre-sale dividend to shareholders even immediately before the business is sold will reduce the effective rate of income tax on the net dividend from 40 per cent to 25 per cent. This requires that the company has retained profits in the company which are eligible for distribution to shareholders as dividends. Also, the acquirer will need to ensure the company makes a cash payment for the advance corporation tax on the dividend, which can be offset in due course against taxable profits generated within the company acquired. Even if the company to be sold does not have the cash to pay a substantial pre-sale dividend, it may be possible to obtain the agreement of the acquirer to loan sufficient cash to allow the dividend to be paid. This can be arranged with adequate protection for the acquirer and should not be ruled out of hand. In return the acquirer should seek some quid pro quo from the vendors.

Another way to reduce the rate of tax from 40 per cent to 25 per cent is by payment of what is called a stock dividend, which is paid in the form of additional shares in the company rather than cash. The advantage to the acquirer is that there will be no advance corporation tax payable.

A buy-back of the shares of the vendor company prior to sale, when classified as 'unapproved' rather than approved for tax purposes, will also effectively reduce the rate of tax from 40 per cent to 25 per cent. Similarly, life interest trusts in which the settler must not be a beneficiary have gains taxed at 25 per cent and not 40 per cent. The tax regulations in these areas are particularly detailed, so expert advice and help with execution are essential.

## 8.8 Earn-out deals

The capital gains tax liability arising from the sale of a company is crystallised on the date of the contract, that is when contracts are exchanged or all conditions precedent are satisfied. In the sale of many private companies, however, not all the purchase consideration is paid at the outset. For example, the total amount of purchase consideration may be agreed, but the vendors may have accepted that some of the payment is to be deferred. More often, deferred consideration arises in earn-out deals and the amount of deferred payment will be dependent on future profit performance during an agreed period.

Earn-out consideration payable by the issue of shares in the acquired company, or other paper instrument such as loan stock, means that the capital gains tax liability is not crystallised until the shares or loan stock are sold for cash. When the earn-out consideration is to be paid in cash, or partly so, a capital gains tax liability will be created on the sale of the business. In these circumstances, the Inland Revenue will seek to include the estimated value of the cash payments and crystallise the corresponding capital gains tax liability.

When the earn-out cash is eventually received, any excess over the estimated value will create an additional tax liability for the vendors. If the amount received is less than the estimated figure, the tax cannot be reclaimed against the original payment because a capital loss cannot be carried back to offset gains in previous years. This means that the estimated value of earn-out payments to be received in cash should be negotiated at the lowest figure acceptable to the Inland Revenue, to avoid a capital loss arising which cannot be offset against the original capital gain.

For example, consider a company sold for £2 million cash and an estimated value of deferred consideration payable in cash of £1 million which is described as the 'right to receive'. The vendors will pay capital gains tax based on the total cash consideration of £3 million, less the indexed value of the shares. If the actual amount of earn-out payment is only £300,000, the tax cannot be clawed back because a capital loss cannot be carried back to a previous tax year. This means that tax has been paid on an estimated gain of £700,000 which never materialised, and can only be used to offset capital gains arising in the current or subsequent years.

## 8.9  Asset sales

From a tax standpoint, an asset sale is generally less favourable to the shareholders of a private company, than the sale of shares, in the UK and most other countries. The vendors will be faced with two tax charges on the sale proceeds. First, there is likely to be a capital gains tax liability faced by the company as a result of selling assets in excess of the allowable cost for tax purposes. If the company has some unutilised capital losses, these could be offset against the capital gains arising on the sale of the assets. Second, the shareholders will be taxed when the cash is extracted from the company.

In most circumstances, acquirers recognise that while they would prefer to buy the assets and the business, they will need to agree to acquire the share capital to achieve tax effectiveness for the vendors. If there are material contingent liabilities or tax irregularities in the company, the acquirer may insist on buying only the assets and the business. The vendors will be faced with a higher tax burden if they wish to sell the business, because in these circumstances the acquirer would not be prepared to make a higher offer to provide recompense to the shareholders.

## 8.10  Trading losses

During recent years, the Inland Revenue has tightened the rules for utilising trading losses. When a company is acquired, a major change in its activities or a reduction in the level of business to a much reduced level during the three years following acquisition is likely to result in the tax losses being disallowed. Equally, the acquirer should seek indemnities from the vendor that similar changes did not occur in the three years before acquisition, because the trading losses will be disallowed and worthless.

The acquisition of the assets and the business, rather than the share capital, will not give the acquirer the tax benefit of any accumulated trading losses, surplus advance corporation tax or capital losses following acquisition. To preserve the trading losses, it is necessary to carry out what is known as a 'hive down'. This involves transferring (hiving down) the business and assets into a new company. Detailed regulations must be followed strictly in order to ensure the tax benefits are preserved.

## 8.11  Tax issues on sale of a subsidiary

It may be possible to transfer the subsidiary being sold to another group subsidiary, which has capital losses available to offset the anticipated capital gains. Detailed taxation rules exist to limit the scope for tax avoidance in this way, and expert advice is essential. Similarly, a pre-sale dividend payment could be tax-effective for a group prior to the sale of a subsidiary.

## 8.12  Key point summary

1. Planning ahead and timely action are needed to minimise and defer capital gains tax liabilities on the sale of a business.
2. Expert tax advice is essential and the arrangements must be implemented meticulously to ensure compliance with the regulations.
3. Valuable retirement relief is available in the UK for shareholders aged 55 or over, employed full time in the business, provided the various conditions are met.
4. The payment of either a pre-completion or stock dividend before legal completion in the UK, in return for a reduced purchase price, achieves worthwhile tax savings.
5. Deferred purchase consideration payable in cash creates a capital gains tax liability on exchange of contracts, but payment in the form of shares or loan stock defers the liability.

# 9 Management buy-outs and buy-ins

When selling to the management team, it is easier to maintain confidentiality compared with selling to a shortlist of prospective buyers. However, there have been instances where the intention to sell has been leaked to the marketplace as a result of a breach of confidentiality within a prospective purchaser's organisation.

The likelihood of a sale being completed to a management buy-out team, once Heads of Agreement have been signed, should be measurably greater than selling to a trade buyer. Although the venture capitalist will require due diligence to be carried out by investigating accountants, there should be no surprises to the management team and, as a result, there should be no case for renegotiating the deal. When selling to a trade buyer, there is always a risk that the due diligence process will reveal something the purchaser regards as material and which the purchaser uses as a basis for renegotiating the deal or withdrawing.

While there are undoubtedly benefits to the vendors from selling to the management team, the orchestration of the sale process needs careful attention. A surprising number of companies have found selling to a management team to be a minefield, because they have assumed that exactly the same process would be appropriate whether or not a management team is involved.

Before allowing the management team to explore the possibility of a buy-out, it needs to be established that:

- the business is suitable for a buy-out;
- the management team are able and willing to make an adequate personal investment;
- the likely deal structure will be acceptable;
- an appropriate sale process and timetable have been defined;
- the sale will be announced in a positive way if the management team buy the business.

## 9.1 Suitable businesses for a management buy-out

During the past decade, more than half of all management buy-outs (MBOs) have involved the disposal of a subsidiary or division. Nearly a quarter of

MBOs have been privately owned businesses. Other sources have included receiverships and privatisation.

### 9.1.1 Sectors

During recent years only about one third of management buy-outs have involved manufacturing businesses. This should dispel the popular myth that the typical MBO is an underperforming manufacturer which is heavily asset-backed.

Financial services and business to business services have represented about one fifth of MBOs. This underlines the fact that while substantial asset-backing is attractive to debt finance providers, a key requirement is adequate cashflow generation.

Some equity investors are shrewd enough to back businesses for the recovery prospects as recession ends. For example, some venture capitalists showed an appetite to invest in construction-related businesses before there was any real evidence of an upturn in the sector.

In addition, there have been hundreds of MBOs in a diverse range of other sectors, and no business sector *per se* is unsuitable for an MBO.

### 9.1.2 Size of business

Since the late 1980s, only about 10 per cent of all MBOs have been deals worth more than £10 million each. These are regarded as 'larger MBOs'. Of these only about six each year on average have been worth more than £100 million. Of the MBOs worth less than £10 million (90 per cent of the total), the average deal size has been under £2 million during the past decade.

### 9.1.3 Key characteristics

The essential ingredients for an MBO are:

- a financially committed and suitably experienced management team;
- a commercially viable business;
- a business which offers an exit opportunity for the equity investors;
- a financeable proposal.

Each of these ingredients is examined in turn.

The management team are the most important ingredient of all. The providers of equity capital have no doubt that they are investing primarily in the management team.

The equity investor will want to be satisfied that the management team are capable of managing and growing the business, without the support of either the parent group or the present shareholders in a private business. More importantly, the investor will want each key member of the management team to be financially and emotionally committed as a result of his or her personal investment to acquire an equity stake in the business. If, for example, the sales and marketing director was not prepared to invest for any reason, this would be a matter of concern to a venture capitalist.

The position of managing director is crucial. Ideally, the existing managing director will be a member of the MBO team, although this may not be the case in a private company. When the incumbent managing director is not part of the MBO team, it is important that the team agree on the choice of managing director at the outset. Ideally, the choice will often be the marketing or sales director, because the MBO will succeed or fail primarily on the ability to win profitable business. The operations, technical, finance or human resources director often has much less relevant experience to be an acceptable managing director.

Cash generation and first-class cash management are essential in every MBO. As part of a group, however, the financial director of a subsidiary may have had virtually no involvement in currency management and other treasury matters such as dealing with banks. Consequently, some equity investors have insisted that a suitably experienced financial director should be appointed who is prepared to invest along with the other managers.

It should be realised that a gap in the management team does not necessarily exclude a buy-out. Some venture capitalists have a register of executives they regard as suitable to join a buy-out or buy-in team, and who have cash available to invest. When a management team are strengthened by an injection of one or more executives in this way, the deal may be referred to as a BIMBO – an unfortunate acronym for buy-in, management buy-out. Even when there is a suitable management team with the exception of a managing director, this does not necessarily rule out a buy-out. Venture capitalists have suitable executives on their register to lead a management team.

If the business is presently making a loss or just breaking even, a recipe of more of the same is unlikely to convince equity investors that an MBO is worth backing. The business plan must outline either new market segments, products, services or distribution channels to be pursued in order to create a growing and profitable business.

Sometimes, the subsidiary or division believes that the elimination of group management charges after the completion of an MBO will improve profit substantially. In a quite typical case, the management team claimed initially that the group charge of about £2 million per annum was exhorbitant. The only services provided by the group were treasury management, legal advice, company secretarial, audit fees and pension administration. This was largely correct, as it would only cost a small fraction of £2 million to provide these services as a separate entity. However, one major point had been ignored: the bulk of the management charge represented a notional charge for the financing cost of the operating assets of the business. When the costs of financing the purchase of the business were taken into account, the saving from escaping the group management charge was modest.

Occasionally, a management team will be invited to pursue an MBO by the current owners because the business is almost certainly unattractive to a trade buyer. The reason could be that, say, 70 per cent of the turnover is with one customer. In the case of a privatisation, the only customer may be the present operating body under government ownership. Under these circumstances, the management team will need to outline to the equity investor how it will win business from other customers in order to reduce the dependence to a commercially acceptable level, and to convince them of their ability to achieve these additional sales. In a privatisation situation, there may be no external sales team, and the management team will have no experience of winning new customers.

Some equity investors in UK MBOs state that they are prepared to hold their investment for the long term. This should not be taken too literally. Venture capitalists prefer to realise their investment by selling their shares within about five years. They are well aware, too, that the evidence demonstrates that they tend to maximise the annual compound rate of return on their investment by selling their shareholding earlier than five years. So when meeting prospective equity investors, management teams should demonstrate an awareness of the marked preference or requirement for many investors to sell their shareholding within that timescale.

The most probable exit opportunities are:

- a sale of the company to a trade buyer, which is likely to be a group listed on either the UK or a foreign stock market;
- a flotation of the business on the stock market, although this is unlikely to make sense unless the market capitalisation is at least £20 million;
- the company may buy out the shareholding of the institutional investor, or even a manager wishing to leave or retire, provided that the business has generated sufficient profit and has adequate cash or borrowing resources.

In a substantial majority of cases, the most likely exit will be a sale of the business to a trade buyer.

For an attractive exit to be achievable, it is important that the business:

- has achieved satisfactory sales and profit performance for at least the preceding two or three years, compared with other companies in the market sector;
- is capable of sustaining sales and profit growth during the medium term;
- is not unduly dependent upon a few of customers;
- has a management team committed to the development of the business.

Consequently, a management team will have to demonstrate how they will achieve continued sales and profit growth throughout the foreseeable future in order to get financial backing.

Equity investors decide to invest because of their assessn
management team, the commercial viability of the business and
hood of a satisfactory exit. When satisfied on these points, howeve
not mean that the investor will be ready to back an MBO at the p
owners are seeking.

The management team need to present profit and cashflow proje ᴐⁿs
over a three-year period. These must take into account the need for:

- fixed asset replacement;
- additional capital expenditure and working capital for growth;
- research and development;
- corporation tax;
- plus a contingency to provide a margin of safety.

The equity investor will want to be satisfied that the management team
will not be asking for additional finance within the medium term, as a result
of an unexpected shortage of cash. On the contrary, they will expect to see
that the generation of profits and cash will enable interest, preference share
dividends and significant repayments of debt finance to be made. As a
consequence, the financial advisers to the management team and the equity
investor will calculate the maximum affordable purchase price to service the
interest cost of debt finance and to provide an acceptable return on the
equity investment.

An MBO is easier to finance if there are substantial tangible assets which
can be charged as security to providers of debt finance. The usual methods
of giving security are:

- a mortgage or a fixed charge on freehold land and buildings or other
  specific fixed assets;
- a floating charge over the business undertaking, including current assets
  such as debtors and stocks.

When the assets available for security are not a substantial part of the purchase price for the MBO, the proportion of ordinary share capital will need
to increase.

## 9.2 Investment by management

Venture capitalists take the view that if the MBO business fails, they want it
to penalise each key member of the team, but not be ruinous to them. They
do not want anyone to be faced with loss of the family home if the MBO
fails.

Typically, each key member of the management team will be required to
invest a minimum of about £25,000, or six months' gross salary. Provided
the personal risk is acceptable, the equity investor will welcome a larger
investment by the management team. In most MBOs, there will be between

three and six key members. It is quite commonplace for the managing director to have the opportunity to invest between one third and one half more than other key team members.

The management team often raise the cash to invest by taking a second mortgage or by borrowing against endowment insurance policies. Sometimes the equity investor will ask the providers of debt finance to arrange suitable mortgages or loans.

Before allowing a management buy-out to commence, it is essential that the group is satisfied that each individual is prepared to invest and is capable of borrowing sufficient cash. In the case of a manager who has negative equity in his or her property, there may be little opportunity to provide security to a lender for investment in the buy-out. Equally, some executives naively think that an investment of £5,000 will be sufficient. It simply is not.

In addition to the key people, there is considerable merit in inviting other managers or fee earners to invest as well. Otherwise there is a risk that a divisive 'them and us' situation could be created between the investing directors and senior and middle managers. Here, a typical investment may be about £5,000 each. In larger MBOs, and in privatisations, it may be appropriate to invite hundreds of staff to invest about £1,000 each.

The mechanism for arranging this sort of investment could be an employee share ownership plan (ESOP). Expert professional advice is needed to establish an ESOP, but the benefits of such a scheme may be worthwhile for the employees. Provision should be made for the disposal and transfer of shares if an employee leaves. Careful tax planning should ensure that interest relief is available for those employees taking out loans to purchase shares wherever possible.

Even if the management team are committed to having managers and staff throughout the business invest in a buy-out, and the group has no objection, it should be made clear to the management team that the intention to pursue a buy-out should be known only to the key members of the team. Otherwise, there may well be a serious distraction and waste of time in the business, as a result of the management team needing to have regular briefing meetings with staff in order to keep them up to date on how the buy-out is progressing. It is quite commonplace in larger buy-outs for the investment by other managers and staff to take place after the buy-out has been completed.

## 9.3 Setting the price

An example illustrates what can go wrong when selling a business to a buy-out team.

A group wished to sell a loss-making engineering component manufacturing business. The written-down value of the net tangible assets was about £9 million, and a key objective for the group was to sell the business without making a book loss. The management team were invited to compete simultaneously with four known trade buyers and were told that the minimum acceptable price would be £10 million, but the group decided not to reveal this figure to the trade buyers. An offer of £8.1 million was made by a venture capitalist on behalf of the management team within about two months. After a further four months, not a single offer has been received from a trade buyer, the key factor being the reluctance to compete against a management team, which could result in buying the business with a demotivated management team, who might leave to pursue a buy-in. Distracted by pursuing the management buy-out and spending time with prospective trade buyers, the losses in the business increased significantly compared with budget. Consequently, the venture capitalist withdrew the original offer and a deal was finally legally completed for £6.9 million.

Listed groups are as prone as private businesses to exaggerate the realisable value of a business to be sold. Valuation should never be carried out in isolation. The number and identity of serious trade buyers must be taken into account. If there is only one serious buyer and a handful of opportunistic acquirers, then the realisable value may be significantly lower than if there are several serious buyers.

As a rule of thumb, if a group wishes to favour a management buy-out team in order to reflect the fact that the chances of achieving legal completion at an agreed figure are significantly higher, the maximum price advantage given to the buy-out team compared to a trade buyer should be 5 per cent of the purchase price. This should not be taken as a recommendation to discount the price to a management team, because listed groups must be seen to have acted in the best interests of the shareholders.

It must be realised that a venture capitalist will not pay the asking price for a business just to win the deal. Venture capitalists calculate the maximum price to be paid in order to give them their required rate of return. Typically, venture capitalists are seeking a compound annual rate of return of between about 28 per cent and 30 per cent pre-tax. This will take into account any dividend or interest income on amounts invested in addition to the capital gain on the shareholding at the time of exit.

The professional advisers to the vendors should have sufficient experience of working with venture capitalists to be able to make an accurate assessment of the likely purchase price payable and an appropriate financing structure of debt and equity which will avoid overburdening the business after the buy-out. If this had been done in the example described earlier, the group wishing to sell the loss-making business would have realised at the outset that there was little chance of avoiding a book loss on the net tangible assets of the business.

It must be realised that many trade buyers will simply not compete with a buy-out team. So it may make sense to set a realistic price for the management team to achieve, based on advice from professional advisers, and to give them about six weeks to submit an outline offer. For the offer to be taken seriously, it should be made in writing by a venture capital firm. If the management team cannot find a venture capitalist to support an offer at the required price, it is reasonable for trade buyers to be pursued without competition from a buy-out team.

## 9.4 Initiating the sale

There are occasions when the group is not prepared to allow a management buy-out to be initiated. For example, the professional advisers may have demonstrated that there is little likelihood of a venture capitalist being able to make an acceptable offer. In such a situation, it is not uncommon for two or three members of the management team to be given a loyalty bonus of between six months' and two years' salary for their help in selling the business. On some occasions, the management team have been allowed to pursue a buy-out and have been assured of a similar loyalty bonus, to ensure their help in selling the business to a trade buyer if they are unable to make an acceptable offer.

The privatisation of public sector businesses usually involves a different set of circumstances. Typically, an information memorandum is made available to prospective purchasers and a firm deadline is set for the receipt of outline written offers. Often, only about 4–6 weeks are allowed for submission of initial written offers from the availability of the information memorandum. In privatisations, it is often much less clear-cut whether or not a management buy-out makes financial sense. The management team may require a feasibility study to be carried out by professional advisers before deciding whether to proceed with a buy-out.

The agency responsible for privatising a business should allow the management team to carry out a feasibility study before the information memorandum is publicly available, and there are precedents where the cost of the feasibility study has been paid by the privatisation agency on behalf of the management team.

More time is often required to submit a written offer from a venture capitalist to purchase a business to be privatised, and it makes sense for the management team to be allowed to initiate the buy-out process, as well as completing the feasibility study, before the information memorandum is made available to trade purchasers.

Perhaps one of the most delicate situations for a group to handle is when a management team request permission to pursue a buy-out and no decision has been made to sell the business. In this situation, the group should say that there is no plan to sell the business and some time will be needed to consider a buy-out. Alternatively, if there is no question of selling the business, the request for a buy-out should be turned down promptly. If the group wishes to consider the unexpected opportunity to sell the business, a similar process of identifying serious buyers and assessing the likely realisable price should be carried out before responding to the management team. In the meantime, it should be pointed out to the management team that they are precluded by law from disclosing any confidential information to an equity investor or provider of debt financing without the express permission of the group. It should be made clear that no work is to be commenced on preparing a business plan to submit to equity investors.

There are situations when a group makes a decision to sell a business, either because it has become non-core or perhaps to reduce unacceptably high gearing, and professional advisers confirm that the only likely buyer is the management team. In these circumstances, some companies have approached three or four venture capitalists in order to agree a deal, before telling the management team that a buy-out opportunity exists. Then the management team would be offered a deal with a particular venture capital company at a previously agreed price. While this process has been followed in only a minority of cases, it offers the advantage to the group that there is no risk of inviting the management team to pursue a buy-out only to find that no acceptable offer is available.

## 9.5 The deal structure

Some groups wrongly assume that the deal structure is irrelevant to them because they believe that the total purchase consideration will be paid in cash on legal completion. This is not necessarily so, and may not be in the best interests of the vendor group.

It should never be overlooked that the prime reason why a venture capitalist invests in a business is the belief that a handsome capital gain will be made by selling it to a trade buyer or obtaining a stock market listing, probably within 3–5 years. Consequently, in larger buy-outs it is not unusual for the vendor group to retain an equity stake in order to enjoy some of the benefit in due course when the management team and venture capitalist achieve a successful exit.

In other cases, the only way to achieve an acceptable offer from a management team has been for the vendor group either to retain a minority equity stake or, less attractively, to accept a partially deferred payment in the form of preference shares or loan stock. When a worthwhile minority equity stake is to be retained, the vendor group should insist on the right to appoint a non-executive director if this is considered desirable.

If the vendor group is to retain a minority equity stake or accept some deferred payment, the financing structure of the deal is important to them. It is essential not only to know the financing structure, but also to be satisfied that the deal structure is not unduly burdensome in terms of interest costs or cashflow requirements. Any covenants to be given to the venture capitalists or debt providers concerning interest cover should be assessed.

## 9.6 Managing the sale process

The issues to be managed include:

- timetable;
- exclusivity;
- cost indemnity;
- negotiating Heads of Agreement;
- warranties and indemnities;
- due diligence;
- announcement and publicity.

Each will be considered in turn.

### 9.6.1 Timetable

Most management buy-outs take longer to legally complete than the group or the management team envisage. Venture capitalists enjoy publishing case histories which show a management buy-out has been legally completed within three months. These are the exceptions. Most management buy-outs take 5–6 months to legally complete. A typical timetable of events is:

Month 1     –   Approval given to pursue a management buy-out.
                –   Management team appoint financial advisers.

Month 2     –   Management write the business plan and financial advisers send it to venture capitalists.
                –   Initial meetings with venture capitalists.
                –   May seek a cost indemnity and period of exclusivity from the group.

Month 3     –   Outline written offers are received from venture capitalists.
                –   Negotiate improved terms from the venture capitalists and appoint the lead investor.

Month 4     –   Group negotiates the sale of the business and signs Heads of Agreement.
                –   Investigating accountants carry out due diligence on behalf of institutional investors.

Months 5/6   –   Lead venture capitalist syndicates equity, if appropriate.
                –   Debt finance arranged.
                –   Legal documents prepared and negotiated.
                –   Legal completion takes place.

Although in the normal course of events it would be early in the third month before outline offers are made by venture capitalists, it is not unreasonable for the vendor group to give only about six weeks for the management team to submit an offer for the business from a venture capitalist, if a decision is to be made on this basis whether or not to allow a management buy-out to proceed. To give the management team, say, three months for a venture capitalist to submit an offer for the business causes undue delay in the sale process, if a decision to involve trade buyers is to be made only when it is known whether or not the management offer is acceptable.

### 9.6.2 Exclusivity

The management team, their professional advisers or the venture capitalist may ask for a period of exclusivity. The purpose is to ensure that the management team are not competing with trade buyers for an agreed period. If the vendor group has decided by the time the request is made to deal only with the management team, a refusal to give a period of exclusivity would seem unnecessarily churlish.

Usually, an initial period of exclusivity would extend to two weeks after the deadline set for the receipt of a written offer for the business from the venture capitalist. This allows sufficient time for face-to-face negotiations to take place after the receipt of the written offer and for Heads of Agreement to be prepared and signed. Obviously, whenever a trade buyer or a management team sign Heads of Agreement they would rightly expect exclusivity to be further extended to two weeks after the planned date for legal completion. A period of two weeks should be sufficient to allow for slippage against the timetable set for legal completion.

### 9.6.3 Cost indemnity

It is commonplace for management teams – or more likely their corporate finance advisers – to ask for a cost indemnity. The fact that such requests are commonplace does not mean that it should be regarded as commonplace to agree. Some companies will not give a cost indemnity to a buy-out team under any circumstances. Others are only prepared to consider a cost indemnity at the point when Heads of Agreement are signed. The decision whether or not, and when, to give a cost indemnity needs an understanding of the situation the management team and the venture capitalist are facing.

It is quite possible that the management team will incur fees of about £5,000, exclusive of disbursements and VAT, if the buy-out is not completed for any reason. This is quite reasonable because corporate finance advisers and venture capitalists realise that it is easy for a management team to pursue a buy-out without real personal commitment if there is no cost penalty to them. So there is a case for the vendor to give a cost indemnity to the management team up to the maximum they will have to pay to their corporate finance advisers if the deal does not legally complete. The decision whether or not to give a cost indemnity should be influenced by whether the management team requested the opportunity to pursue a buy-out or if they were invited to do so by the vendor group. Clearly, if the management team were invited to pursue a buy-out, they have stronger grounds for expecting a request for a cost indemnity to be accepted.

The other advisers to the management team will include tax advisers, and solicitors to handle their agreement with the venture capitalist. It is quite probable that the solicitors will be prepared to work on a contingent fee only basis. On the other hand, it is likely that the tax advisers will expect a commitment to pay at least a reduced fee if the deal is not completed for any reason. So there is a case for an increased cost indemnity to be provided to the management team once Heads of Agreement have been signed.

When Heads of Agreement have been signed, the lead venture capitalist will quickly incur significant costs for professional work to be carried out. Typically these will include:

- lawyers to handle their agreement with the buy-out team and the Sale and Purchase Agreement to buy the business;
- advice on the prospects for the industry sector and a strategic assessment of the business to be purchased;
- investigating accountants to carry out the due diligence;
- tax, pensions and property advice, as appropriate.

There will be only limited scope for the lead venture capitalist to have the above advice provided on a contingent fee basis. Consequently, the venture capitalist may press extremely hard for a cost indemnity to protect against the situation in which the vendor unilaterally withdraws from the sale or attempts to renegotiate the deal on more favourable terms. Not surprisingly, the response from vendors differs widely.

Where the vendor takes the transaction to the venture capitalists first and only invites the management team to pursue a buy-out on previously agreed terms, there have been cases of larger buy-outs where the cost indemnity was more than £1 million. It has to be assumed, however, that the cost indemnity was agreed as an integral part of the negotiations to strike an acceptable purchase price and deal. At the other end of the spectrum, there are some companies that are adamant that they will never give a cost indemnity to a venture capitalist.

### 9.6.4 Negotiating Heads of Agreement

A vendor should never negotiate the sale of the business directly with the management team, and there should be no difficulty, in practice, in following this advice. It is strongly recommended that an outline written offer is received either from the venture capitalist or from the corporate finance adviser to the management team, on behalf of a named venture capitalist, before agreeing to negotiate the Heads of Agreement. More importantly, the negotiations should be led by the venture capitalist or by the corporate finance adviser to the management team, with a representative of the management merely in attendance. Even so, these negotiations may become emotionally charged and as a result it is not unusual for the vendor to have the negotiations led by financial advisers.

At the outset of any negotiations, the venture capitalist should be asked directly the extent of any need to syndicate equity. If this is envisaged, the venture capitalist should be asked to what extent other equity investors have been sounded out on a 'no names' basis. Equally, the venture capitalist should be asked what preparatory work has been done to secure the debt financing required.

It is not enough for the vendor group to assume that equity syndication and raising of debt are not a problem for them. It has been known for a venture capitalist to request a lower price or retention of equity or some deferred payment only shortly before legal completion, because the equity and debt financing has not gone as well as expected. It is important that the vendor group makes it quite clear at the outset that once the price and terms have been agreed in the Heads of Agreement, no changes in the deal will be acceptable. It is too late to make this point if shortly before legal completion the venture capitalist demands that the terms are renegotiated to prevent the deal falling through.

### 9.6.5 Warranties and indemnities

Vendors tend to assume that because the management team have been managing the business, they will not be expected to provide any warranties and indemnities. This is definitely not the case. In many groups, matters affecting freeholds, leasehold properties, intellectual property, taxation, litigation, risk and foreign currency management are handled by group staff. Without question, the vendor group will be required to give adequate warranties and indemnities on these matters.

Furthermore, if the venture capitalist is paying a price for the business comparable to that of a trade buyer, there is a strong case for expecting to receive comparable warranties and indemnities. The fact that the management team are familiar with the commercial and operational activities of the business does not negate the case for expecting warranties from the vendor group. Obviously, the individual members of the management buy-out team are unlikely to have significant personal assets with which to meet any warranty or indemnity claims from the venture capitalist. Also, the management team are never asked to give warranties and indemnities to a trade buyer. So, every vendor should realise that reasonable warranties and indemnities must be given.

### 9.6.6 Due diligence

While the venture capitalist chooses to invest primarily in the calibre and experience of the management team, the decision to invest is taken only on completion of the due diligence process and after any strategic assessment of the sector and the business is carried out. Vendor groups must realise that the scope and rigour of due diligence carried out will be comparable to that carried out by a prospective trade buyer. Any refusal to co-operate with the people carrying out the due diligence and any strategic appraisal is likely to result in the purchase process being terminated. Equally, if any material factors are revealed, which had not been known or anticipated by the management team and communicated to the venture capitalist, the vendor should expect the venture capitalist to renegotiate the deal in the same way a trade buyer would.

### 9.6.7 Announcement and publicity

The audience for announcing that a management buy-out has been completed is basically the same one as would apply for a sale of the business to a trade buyer, namely:

*Shareholders*

The press release, and any Stock Exchange circular required, needs to demonstrate to shareholders, the Stock Exchange and financial journalists that the group has acted in the best interests of the shareholders.

*Other group employees*

The internal announcement should not encourage any false impression that other buy-outs will be welcome or acceptable.

*Customers and suppliers*

It is quite possible that other group subsidiaries will continue to do business with customers and suppliers of the buy-out business. Consequently, it is important that these customers and suppliers should learn of the buy-out from the vendor.

If the vendor group has retained a minority equity stake or accepted some deferred purchase consideration, the success of the business is important to the group. Where a minority equity stake has not been retained, it is important to avoid adverse publicity caused by an early sale to a trade buyer at a very attractive price. When this happens, investors and journalists alike have good reason for being critical of the vendor group. Similarly, if a stock market flotation is achieved within, say, 18 months of the buy-out at a much improved valuation, criticism from journalists and shareholders should be expected. It is reasonable to ask why the vendor group did not pursue a sale or stock market flotation, with a retention of an equity stake, rather than a management buy-out.

## 9.7 Key point summary

1. Vendors must ensure that an MBO is demonstrably feasible before allowing the management team to pursue one.
2. Venture capitalists require an experienced management team, with each person prepared to invest cash in the business.
3. Vendors need to realise that some trade buyers will not compete against a management team, and organise the sale process accordingly.
4. Venture capitalists will require certain warranties and indemnities from the vendor.
5. Management teams should recognise that most venture capitalists seek to realise their equity investment within 3–5 years, by a sale or a stock market flotation.

# Index